DRACULA
a feminist revenge fantasy, really.
by Kate Hamill
based loosely on the novel by Bram Stoker

DRACULA
Copyright © 2022 Kate Hamill
ALL RIGHTS RESERVED

COPYRIGHT NOTICE:
This Play is fully protected under the copyright laws of the United States of America and all countries covered by the International Copyright Union (including the British Commonwealth, Canada, Australia), the Berne Convention, the Pan-American Copyright Convention, and the Universal Copyright Convention, as well as all countries throughout the world with which the United States has reciprocal copyright relations. All rights, including but not limited to professional, amateur, and educational stage rights, motion picture, recitation, lecturing, public reading, radio broadcasting, television, video, YouTube, Zoom or any such Internet service or transmission, or sound recording, all other forms of mechanical or electronic reproduction, such as CD-ROM, CD-I, DVD, information storage and retrieval systems and photocopying, and the rights of translation into foreign languages, are strictly reserved. No part of this book may be reproduced, or transmitted in any form, by any means, now known or yet to be invented, without the prior written permission of TRW Plays in its capacity as publisher.

SPECIAL NOTE ON SONGS AND RECORDINGS:
For the performance of copyrighted songs, arrangements or recordings as mentioned or contained in this Play, the permission of the copyright owner(s) must be obtained by You prior to their use. If You are unable to secure permission from the copyright owner(s), other songs, arrangements or recordings may be substituted provided You obtain permission from the copyright owner(s) of such songs, arrangement or recordings. Furthermore, songs, arrangements or recordings in the public domain, which are no longer governed by copyright and do not require permission for their use, may be substituted. Any substitution by You of the songs, arrangements or recordings as found in the Play must reflect the intention of the Author with respect to style, theme and content.

PERFORMANCE WARNING and ADVISORY:
Professional, amateur, and educational groups are hereby advised that performance of this Play requires a license and is subject to payment of a royalty whether or not admission is charged. The stage performance rights throughout the world for this Play are controlled exclusively by TRW Plays. No professional, amateur, or educational performance may be given without obtaining, in advance of any and all performances, the

written permission of TRW Plays and paying the requisite fee. Current royalty rates and performance information may be found at our website at www.trwplays.com and www.trwplays.co.uk. Inquiries concerning all other rights should be forwarded on to:

TRW Plays
A division of Theatrical Rights Worldwide
1180 Avenue of the Americas, 6th Floor
New York, NY 10036
trwplays@theatricalrights.com

and

TRW Plays
A division of Theatrical Rights Worldwide
19 Margaret Street, 3rd Floor
London W1W 8RR UK
trwplays@theatricalrights.co.uk

TRW Plays ATTRIBUTION:
Professional, amateur, and educational licensees shall include the following notice in all programs, advertisements, and other printed material distributed or published in connection with the production of the Play:

DRACULA
is produced by special arrangement with TRW Plays.
www.trwplays.com
www.trwplays.co.uk

Printed in the U.S.A. / U.K.
ISBN: 978-1-63852-139-6

The world premiere production of *Dracula (a feminist revenge fantasy, really.)* was produced by Classic Stage Company; John Doyle, Artistic Director, on February 17th, 2020. It was directed by Sarna Lapine; Brian Eckert was assistant director; the scenic design was by John Doyle; the costume design was by Robert Perdziola, the lighting design was by Adam Honoré, the sound design was by Leon Rothenberg, the dramaturg was Kristin Leahey, the dialect coach was Jane Guyer Fujita, the fight director was Michael G. Chin, the props supervisor was Carrie Mossman, the production stage manager was by Sarah E.T. Jackson, the assistant production stage manager was Giles T. Horne, and the assistant to the playwright was Kelly Letourneau. Casting director for the world premiere was by Karyn Casl.

The cast was as follows (in alphabetical order):

DRACULA	Matthew Amendt
DRUSILLA/MERCHANT/MILLER	Laura Baranik
JONATHAN HARKER	Michael Crane
MINA HARKER	Kelley Curran
DOCTOR VAN HELSING	Jessica Frances Dukes
RENFIELD	Kate Hamill
MARILLA/MAID	Lori Laing
LUCY WESTENRA	Jamie Ann Romero
DOCTOR GEORGE SEWARD	Matthew Saldivar

> "god should have made girls lethal
> when he made monsters of men"
>
> —Elisabeth Hewer

Character Breakdown
(6 women, 3 men)

WOMEN:
1. Doctor Van Helsing
2. Mina Harker
3. Lucy Westenra
4. Marilla / Maid
5. Drusilla / Merchant / Miller
6. Renfield

MEN:
1. Dracula
2. Jonathan Harker
3. Doctor George Seward

Women

1. DOCTOR VAN HELSING: 40s+. American. A female vampire hunter. She takes no nonsense from anybody. She wears dusty beaten clothing and a big cowboy hat. She has a long nasty old scar all up and down the side of her face, as if someone has taken their hand and RIPPED down, long ago. It's from an encounter she'd rather not talk about. She's been through it. She's a bit of a know-it-all; okay, she's a lot of a know-it-all. She's prickly. She's strong. She's brilliant. She's no Lady. She's on the hunt. She is badass—and 19th century men do not, as a rule, appreciate it.

2. MINA HARKER: 20s-30s. Very smart. Caring. Loyal. Wants to do the right thing. Was raised to be a Lady, and is thus suppressing an inner fire that emerges throughout the progression of the play. Great emotional depth, good sense of humor. Must face her darkest fears—comes out stronger at the end of it. Secretly an adventurer, and fighter. Is called to be more than she once was.

3. LUCY WESTENRA: 20s-30s. Bright, funny, vivacious, playful, and mischievous. Feels trapped and torn by expectations. About to be married, and deeply conscious of how that puts her under a 19th century man's control. Reflexively flirtatious. Believes she must pretend to be less than she is. Yearns for freedom. Falls desperately ill after being bitten by Dracula... and then becomes a completely different being—an animalistic vampire demon—a naturally

manipulative predator. Lucy's vampire self is deeply unpredictable and frightening.

4. MARILLA / as cast: 20s-30s. A vampire. More animal than human. Was lured into vampirehood by Dracula, who then proceeded to exploit her. Enjoys being a predator. Finds pleasure in consuming others. Resents her objectification. Manipulative; vicious; probably sociopathic. Capable of moving very fast—blink, and *oh God*, she's right behind you. Sister-wife to DRUSILLA. Doubles with MAID—an underpaid, resentful servant.

5. DRUSILLA / as cast: 20s-30s. A vampire. More animal than human. Was lured into vampirehood by Dracula, who then proceeded to exploit her. Enjoys being a predator. Finds pleasure in consuming others. Resents her objectification. Manipulative; vicious; probably sociopathic. Capable of moving very fast—blink, and *oh God*, she's right behind you. Sister-wife to MARILLA. Doubles with MILLER—a casually brutal asylum attendant, and MERCHANT—a merchant looking to make a sale.

6. RENFIELD: any age. A madwoman. Worships Dracula. Believes that if she can earn his approval, she will be free. Not a bad soul, really, but capable of extreme brutality or duplicity in service of her religious zealotry. Almost a child, in her way.

Men

1. DRACULA / as cast: late 30s-late 50s. A physically imposing man. He is... extremely confident. Strong. Funny. Charming. Sexy. You'd like him, reader—no, really, you would. He makes people lose their heads. Manipulative. Commanding. Capable of being very, very frightening. Unpredictable. Physically strong. Incredible with language. Unimaginably powerful. Brilliant. Casually takes pleasure in cruelty. An equal-opportunity sexual sadist. A toxic predator; a wolf in the fold; a very old and clever parasite, capable of adapting and surviving. Fundamentally enjoys himself.

2. JONATHAN HARKER: 20s-40s. A nice man. A truly decent man. A lawyer; a man of letters; a slight man; a slightly fussy man. If being unkind, one could say he's delicate. He's very, very British. Cares about people. Is maybe a little rule-bound. Loves his wife, Mina, deeply. Is bitten by Dracula, and then loses his mind—becoming an

easily-confused, raving shambles. After recovering from sickness, he slowly gives in to Dracula's darkness—becoming an abusive, toxic man. Once he's under Dracula's influence, we can't always tell if he's telling the truth. Can quickly switch from likable to extremely volatile.

3. DOCTOR GEORGE SEWARD: 30s-40s. The head physician of a lunatic asylum. A good man, but starts out the play as a product of his era—has some trouble listening to women. Believes only in the evidence of his own eyes. Tends to mansplain. Deeply in love with his fiancé Lucy Westenra, of whom he is overprotective. Has a very contentious relationship with Van Helsing. Doesn't like to not feel in control. Chivalrous. Thinks of himself as a modern man; a man of science. Over the course of the play, he learns to accept female leadership and question his assumptions. A brave man. Likeable.

Notes from the Playwright

It is my preference that the entirety of the ensemble begin the play in whites and creams, so that as blood is spilled, it becomes increasingly messy—the whites and creams are stained with blood, sprayed and spattered. By the end, everyone is polluted. All costumes and scenery and setting should be gestural, rather than literal. Keep it extremely simple and swift-moving. It could almost be set now—the scenery may all come from the madhouse.

There is no point in doing a vampire play if you can't have fun in doing so. If you explore the glee, the darkness will also pop.

The vampires in this play do not have fangs; they are not pale and drawn; they are not abnormal physically in any way. *The monsters look just like us.*

Please attack all text at the speed of thought.

*This play is dedicated to the late Terry Teachout,
a true champion of the arts and artists.*

ACT ONE

PROLOGUE

Two scenes happen simultaneously: in one, Mina says goodbye to her husband, Jonathan; in the other, Dr. Seward's asylum, Renfield sits, humming to herself. She may have been doing so as the audience enters. She is taking a teacup and carefully crushing sugar cubes into powdered sugar. She is extremely dirty, and wears no shoes. She is happy. She spreads the powdered sugar out on a flat surface, and waits, expectantly, staring into the air—happily humming. At some point—the audience need not all be seated—she furtively—looking around to see if anyone might see her—digs out a bit of chalk... and finishes writing the end of the following poem on the wall of her cell. **PLEASE NOTE:** *we must be able to see & read this poem throughout each of Renfield's scenes, if not the entire play.*

Our Father
Who art in Earth
Of Earth
And by Earth
Hallowed be Thy Name.
Thy Kingdom Come
Thy will be done
On Earth, in perpetuity
Give us this day
~~**Our daily bread**~~
What we deserve
And forgive us our trespasses
~~**As we**~~
And crush those who drain
Our lives away from us.
Lead us not into temptation
But deliver us ~~**from ev**~~
From bondage:

> For thine is my kingdom, and my power
> And glory, forever.
> And ever
> And ever
> happily ever after
> *(written upside down and backwards)* **Amen.**
>
> **P.S. I Love You.**
> **Your Renfield**

> *As Renfield conducts her strange little rituals in the corner:*

MINA:
I wish you could take me with you.

JONATHAN:
I might, if it weren't—

MINA:
Weren't for my condition, I know.
You are being overprotective.

JONATHAN:
It is my right.

MINA:
That doesn't mean you are *in* the right.

JONATHAN:
We've been over this, Mina.

> *Beat.*

MINA:
—You shall come back to find me—a cranky, bloated, old cow!

JONATHAN:
I cannot wait. *(he kisses her)* That's the coach.

MINA
Jonathan—you will take care of yourself?

JONATHAN:
(in a rush to leave)—yes.

MINA:
And write to me every day, and tell me of your adventures—since I cannot have them myself?

JONATHAN:
—yes.

MINA:
And you will be good, won't you?

JONATHAN:
Noooo—

> *She hits him.*

—yesyes, of course!

> *Mina kisses him—he exits—and then stands for a moment, rubbing her stomach—it is early days—and then sighs, frustrated:*

JONATHAN (O/S):
Mina! I'm going to be late!

MINA:
(resigning herself) Coming, dear.

> *Mina exits.*

1.

Renfield's work done, she surveys it for a moment, beaming, proud—then hides away the chalk again. She sits by the spread sugar, humming, patiently. The buzz of a fly—she watches it, then turns to the audience:

RENFIELD:
One of my first memories
Of my self
Before I even knew there is a self
to forget—
I was 2 years old,
Or 3—practically a precious infant.
It was late at night—*so* late and *so* dark.
I had been out with my parents
Far past my bedtime.
I had fallen asleep in the carriage.
And my father picked me up
To bring me into the house.
The instant he lifted me,
I woke up!
But I knew
That if I opened my eyes—
I should be made to walk on my own.
So I kept them squeezed tight
Because it felt—
Magical, like flying,
To be carried, gently
In his strong arms
Towards my home.

His strength was my strength
I could go limp
And weak and soft, secure
That Daddy would never—
Ever happily everAFTER ever
let me fall!

And THAT'S how it is.

When he takes you!

It's not *scary*, it's not—
It doesn't feel *bad*, you don't—
Have to *worry*, you can—
Let all of your worries melt away!
Daddy is here, Daddy's in charge!
And if you trust in him, you too
May be delivered!

> *She is hurt by the lack of response.*

You say I'm mad, but—
All prophets are thought mad in their day!

> *Getting angry and hostile.*

So laugh if you want, stare—turn up your noses, you bad brats—
I am his most beloved child, and
You'll answer for schoolyard bullying, you—
disobedient—CHITS!

> *Singing a la schoolyard.*

You're going to be so sorrryyyy
You're going to be in trouble—

> *No longer singing.*

When Our Father comes! And—

> *The exact sound children make when someone goes to the principal's office.*

Ooooohhhh.
—Daddy is coming.

The buzz of a fly—and Renfield suddenly SLAPS her hand down on the sugar. She looks down—cups her hand—and pops the fly into her mouth. She chews and grimaces; it is not pleasant for her.

—Just practicing.

2.

Just outside a castle, present-day Romania. It is an extremely bright, sunny day.

A moment. Two. Flies buzz. Maybe some birds caw.

And then—we hear heavy breathing. Jonathan Harker is dragging up a heavy trunk to the doors of the castle. It's hot, and he's been dragging this thing for a mile—he's not accustomed to physical effort. Jonathan Harker is a lawyer; a man of letters; slight man. He's very, very British. And right now, he's at his wit's end. He finishes dragging up the trunk. He wipes his brow with a handkerchief, tries to make himself presentable. When he puts his handkerchief back in his pocket, his hand catches on—a necklace of some kind. He looks at it, is annoyed with himself—puts it back in his pocket. The audience need not see what it is.

He squints up at the castle, in that scorching sun. Not knowing quite what to do, he looks around—no sign of life. Finally, hesitating, he decides to knock on the great doors. This makes him feel rather stupid. Nobody answers. He knocks again. Nobody answers. This makes him feel even more stupid. He clears his throat.

JONATHAN:
H—hello?
Hello?

> *Nothing. The caw of birds: **caw, caw**.*

It's Jonathan Harker.
I said, it's Jonathan Harker!!!!—Esquire?!!!

> ***Caw caw caw—***
> *and he's pretty much monologuing to himself.*

7

I've come here—all the way from London!
To—godforsaken—middle of nowhere, bloody Eastern Europe—and I've been traveling for—forever—ship to train to coach to—to—to *(the biggest outrage of all)* FOOT—
Because the peasants—suppose that's not the word, anymore—local chaps—my porters, who were quite expensive, by the way—ABANDONED me a mile down the road! And I have these—legal papers—and they are heavy, and it's HOT out, and I am obviously here on a fools' errand and will probably DIE abandoned in—in Romania, or wherever it is—***(CAW CAW CAW CAW)*** eaten by <u>birds</u> ***(hungry CAWWWW)!***

He bangs on the door frantically.

HELLO?!! IS ANYBODY HOME? HELLO?!!!!

The door suddenly swings open. A big man stands there, dressed plainly; nothing special in his attire, except perhaps that it is spotless. He has, at this point, a rather strong patrician Romanian accent. He smiles. His teeth are so white.

DRACULA:
Hello!

JONATHAN:
Oh!—you—scared me, sir.
I was beginning to think there wasn't a living soul in the place!

The man smiles.

My name is Jonathan Hark—

DRACULA:
Mister Jonathan Harker. Of *(jovially)* Londinium, Britannia. Angalo-land. I know.

JONATHAN:
(unnerved) How—do you—know?

DRACULA:
You were shouting it at the doors!

JONATHAN:
Yes. Well,—it has been—a long journey, and my porters left (me)

DRACULA:
I *know.*
Again—*shouting.*

Jonathan tries to recover his dignity.

JONATHAN:
I'm to be taken inside at once. I am a solicitor—

DRACULA:
Ahhh—

JONATHAN:
—come to this country on behalf of my firm—

DRACULA:
Ohhh—

JONATHAN:
To arrange the Count's purchase of property in Britain!

DRACULA:
OoOooo!

The Count smiles.

JONATHAN:
If you would be good enough—as to call some servants for my trunk!

DRACULA:
No need, Mister Jonathan Harker—Esquire.

He happily strides over to the trunk and lifts it—like it is NOTHING—like it's a featherweight—over his shoulder.

JONATHAN:
My heavens, man, you are—*(his voice squeaks a little)* Strong.

DRACULA:
Yes. *(he bounces the trunk happily)* I am.

JONATHAN:
When shall I be taken to the Count?

DRACULA:
You are taken already!

JONATHAN:
Wha—/

DRACULA:
/—I am Count Dracula.

> *Jonathan stumbles back as a bird CAW CAW CAWS.*

Do enter, friend Jonathan.

> *Jonathan, taken aback, backs through the great doors and disappears. The Count remains behind for a moment. Jovially.*

Ahhh—what a beautiful, sunny day.

> *He savors the light, opens his mouth in that terrible grin, as if to eat the sun—feel it—ravens **caw**; and the Count turns and disappears into the darkness.*

3.

Inside the castle. It is dark, dark, cold and dark. Cold wet stone everywhere. The Count and Jonathan sit at a table. And in the corners—are 2 women: Drusilla and Marilla. Like servants, they lay before Jonathan a lovely meal; too much food for one person. They hold decanters and stand in the corners, like extremely unhappy caterers. They are NOT wearing enough clothing. Jonathan tries hard not to stare. They do not smile. They are angry. One pours a cup of wine for him—Jonathan stares at her—and then, overcome, violently <u>sneezes.</u> She stares at him, dead-eyed, and backs away to the corner.

JONATHAN:
I do beg your pardon, sir—but it is—rather musty in here.

DRACULA:
"Musty."
This castle is—an ancient, sacred site. It has been in the family for centuries.

JONATHAN:
Oh? I am quite interested in the local history, you know—actually, as I was traveling, I heard the most fascinating sort of—folklore, about this place, (and I)—

DRACULA:
—eat, friend Jonathan.

JONATHAN:
(gesturing at the food) Is all of this for me?

DRACULA:
I have dined already.

Marilla makes an aggrieved "ar-hrm" sound; the Count glares at her, and she subsides.

JONATHAN:
—Shouldn't—the ladies—like to join?

DRACULA:
What *ladies?*

JONATHAN:
Uhm—

DRACULA:
Who, *them?* They are not hungry.

> *Drusilla makes an even more aggrieved sound; the Count gives her the Death Eye. The Count pointedly snaps his fingers. He beckons to Drusilla; she is obliged to stand in front of him; her face is like stone.*

They are only here—for you to look at, Jonathan Harker. Do you not like to look upon them?

JONATHAN:
—I am married, sir.

DRACULA:
Your wife is not present, man! You may look your fill. You may—even—touch.

> *Dracula snaps—and Marilla is obligated to stand near Jonathan. She stares at Jonathan. Her eyes are full of cold death. Her lips curl in a sneer, even as she submits. Somewhere inside of her, an animal paces.*

JONATHAN:
(Marilla moves towards him—he is so very British) Um—No.

DRACULA:
Truly?

JONATHAN:
Yes. I mean NO. Thank You.

DRACULA:
Ah—such—a *nice* man. *(observing Jonathan rather like a strange insect)* Such lovely—modern manners.

JONATHAN:
(clearing throat) If—if your ancestors have lived here for so long, Count, what makes you wish to move to Britain?

DRACULA:
(he releases Drusilla with a smack on the butt; she retreats) I'm afraid the times are changing,—even in thi*s musty* land; and what was once held as sacred is—defiled. Ancient hierarchies are being discarded. Revolution—is on every tongue.
It is no longer safe to stand above the crowd— and I have not lived so long because I am short-sighted.

JONATHAN:
And here I thought—you might just—wish a change of climate!

DRACULA:
(not laughing) Ha. Ha. Haaaaaa.
If control is shifting to the masses, than I must be of the masses. I must not rule from a castle on the hill anymore. Instead, I must become a common man, anonymous;—welcomed everywhere, and remembered nowhere.
A man—rather—like you. *(he points at Jonathan; maybe he even lays a finger on him)*

JONATHAN:
(starting back from the finger) Me?

DRACULA:
(he smiles) But inside—*(he taps his chest)*—always *boyar.*

JONATHAN:
—*Boyar?*

DRACULA:
"Master."

Jonathan pulls out a little notebook to write it down.

JONATHAN:
—I did make a—study—of the local language before I came!

DRACULA:
As I study your English—your speech!
Study you.

JONATHAN:
(he laughs nervously) I've heard some words—in your country, that I never encountered in my books. Would you be so good as to translate?

Dracula smiles that charming smile and nods.

"Pokol?"

DRACULA:
"Hell."

JONATHAN:
"Ordog"

DRACULA
"Demon."

JONATHAN:
And—"Vrolok?"

DRACULA:
Vrolok: many translations, over the years! *Shtriga* when the Turks occupied this land, *wapier* in medieval Poland. To the west, in these heretical times: *das WAMPIR.*
Vampire.
But you knew that, Jonathan Harker.

JONATHAN:
—What?

DRACULA:
Have... naughty children—been telling you some nasty rumors?

JONATHAN:
Well—ah—the—the local—

DRACULA:
Peasants?

JONATHAN:
Is that—the term anymore?
—Those—"folks"—had—bizarre notions; funny, really—about, um. What happens. In this place.

DRACULA:
Naughty, naughty. They must be dealt with. *(he nods to the women, who stir eagerly, restlessly)*

JONATHAN:
I don't want to—start any trouble. I only was—wondering—why they are so frightened?

DRACULA:
(shrugging) Ghost stories. Folk legends. Fairy tales.
But you are a modern man, Jonathan Harker. Do you really give credence to filthy superstitions? *(he is getting closer and closer)* Do you believe that—you are now—in the presence of *monsters?*

There is tension, the women's hackles are rising—then suddenly Dracula pounds the table.

FEE FI FO FUM, I SMELL THE BLOOD OF AN ENGLISHMUN! Eh??? EH???

Dracula laughs and laughs and pounds Jonathan's back chummily.

JONATHAN:
Hahaha. Ha. *(the back pounding has reached a pitch)* Ow.

DRACULA:
(cutting off his laughter instantly) I do not wish to speak anymore of this old Transylvania, full of blasphemous rabble. I wish to talk of life in my soon-new home!

He snaps his fingers—Marilla resentfully fills Jonathan's cup; he tries not to look at her.

Tell me all about Britannia—its customs, its people!
Tell me of your wonderful wife, who inspires such *fidelity.*
What is her name?

JONATHAN:
—Mina.

DRACULA:
Charming Mina Harker. Where is she now? Curled up in cozy Londinium?

JONATHAN:
She is—visiting a school friend, in Whitby, on the coast.

DRACULA:
(sitting up) Sleeping over with a schoolgirl friend! What is this fresh young chum's name?

JONATHAN:
—Miss Lucy Westenra.

DRACULA:
Miss! Miss is better than Mrs.

JONATHAN:
Pardon?

DRACULA:
Used goods are not my taste! *(he slaps Drusilla's butt; she looks ready to kill)* Give me a plump virgin any day of the week. *(he laughs)*

JONATHAN:

(standing up) Sir!

> *He stands and is ready to leave.*

I'm afraid I must bid you good night.
And I pray we may—confine ourselves to business, in the morning!

> *He begins to leave.*

DRACULA:

Men love to talk so, Jonathan Harker.
Of wives and business and civilized doings.
But we may know him—by his acts!

> *He winks at him.*
>
> *Jonathan exits. Dracula chuckles—the women, like hounds on a scent, follow after Jonathan—then look at each other:*

4.

A small room in Dracula's castle. Jonathan is finishing a letter by candlelight. He signs it, then looks around: somewhere, wolves are howling. It is cold in this room; he does not want to take off his clothes. In fact, he picks up his jacket; he feels something in the pocket, and considers putting it on—but does not, pats it instead. He is trying, hard, not to give in to superstition. He only has the one small candle, and it is very dark. He shivers, and then crawls into the bed, and pulls the jacket over him. He does not want to pray, but finally:

JONATHAN:
Our Father, who art in Heaven—

The wolves howl. He finishes the rest of the prayer silently. He blows out the candle. A moment of absolute darkness. We do not know how long it lasts; perhaps, somewhere, there is a little rustling—light; it could be clothes, or tiny wings—and then, in the dark:

MARILLA:
(mocking) Our Father—

DRUSILLA:
(mocking) Our Father—

They laugh, throatily. A noise of pure, absolute terror from Jonathan—and snap, the lights come on—Marilla is holding his arms. Drusilla sits on his legs. He is pinned down, and powerless. Drusilla and Marilla are no longer scantily dressed. In fact, they are in shapeless, long, covering sweaters—maybe ratty and stained, but very much what women wear when at home and trying to impress NO ONE. <u>They wear these for the rest of the play.</u>

DRUSILLA:
What a *nice* man.

17

MARILLA:
Your father can't help you now!

Jonathan makes a little sound.

DRUSILLA:
Shh, shh.

MARILLA AND DRUSILLA:
SHHHHHHHH.

When he looks into their eyes, he is suddenly transfixed—like prey. He is totally under their spell; he lies transfixed. They stroke him, smiling.

MARILLA:
Do you know, little man—when I was taken by the Count
Many centuries ago—
There was a famine
In my country

DRUSILLA:
There was a war in mine.
Too many children—and
My parents sold me
To save their sons—

MARILLA:
I had seen my family perish—
Their bones sticking from their skin—
And I myself, the strongest of them all—
was starving, close to death—

DRUSILLA:
And I had been passed
From master to master—
Used until I could work no more—

MARILLA AND DRUSILLA:
And the Count came to me and said:

MARILLA:
Come with me, and you will never go hungry—

DRUSILLA:
Come with me, and you will never be powerless!

MARILLA AND DRUSILLA:
Drink of this blood, eat of this body—

DRUSILLA:
And all your struggles will be over!

MARILLA:
If the choice is
Consume or be consumed...

DRUSILLA:
Fee fi fo fum!

They hiss as their teeth come in.

DRUSILLA:
We are kinder than our husband, mortal.

MARILLA:
You shall not suffer long.

Jonathan tries one last time to struggle, but—

DRUSILLA AND MARILLA:
Shhhhhhhhhh.

He is transfixed again, like a mouse before snakes; they are excited; and Jonathan—is completely under their spell; they nuzzle him; their teeth are so sharp.

DRUSILLA:
It's your own fault, darling—

MARILLA:
Coming in here—

DRUSILLA:
Dressed like that—

MARILLA:
Looking so good!

DRUSILLA:
(they are much stronger than he is) Don't you want us to make you feel

MARILLA:
(he's like a little rag doll) Like the big strong man you are—

DRUSILLA:
You know you want it:

DRUSILLA AND MARILLA:
Give it up, now,—
Give in to us—
GIVE IT—

> *They, smiling, move in to bite him:*

DRACULA:
(*he has appeared from nowhere*) BACK!

> *They suddenly recoil—hissing—they are purely animal, now—*

BACK!

> *He throws them off of Jonathan, who is frozen.*

OFF!
He is not for you!

> *One of them feints back, and he stops her, <u>very</u> peevish.*

What did I say?!!!

> *Any sexiness is now gone; the women are past pissed-off.*

DRUSILLA:
You SAID we would be free—and yet we serve!

MARILLA:
You SAID we would never go hungry—and yet we starve!

DRACULA:
So you wish to end—pitchforks and torches, at the hands of a mob? Do you not want to see a new land, full of new peoples—new, delicious peoples?

MARILLA:
A land full of "plump virgins", husband?

DRUSILLA:
Do you seek a new wife in this Britannia? You cannot feed the ones you have!

> *He advances on her—and she shrinks, hissing.*

DRACULA:
Do I find rebellion—even in my own nest?!

> *He gets close, closing down on her throat—and then strokes her face. She is frozen.*

Do not forget who is Master, here!!!

He pushes her violently away.

MARILLA:

(desperately) We cannot sleep for hunger!

DRACULA:

Blah blah blah blah. Such *melodrama*.

> *He sighs, exasperated—reaches into the darkness, and pulls out a sack. It is moving. Harshly:*

Split it.

> *They jump to it; again, they are animals—Dracula moves over Jonathan.*

Oh, friend Jonathan. In these *musty* aged castles, full of old sins—

MARILLA:

(disappointed) It's so small!

DRACULA:

What dark ancestral nightmares may creep into a modern man's head!

> *The women are deeply bummed out by their meal. Dracula mesmerizes Jonathan.*

DRUSILLA:

(sighing mightily) Do you want the front end or the back?

DRACULA:

You have only been dreaming, Englishmun.
Close your eyes.

> *Drusilla shrugs, making a face—and shakes the sack, testing it like a good melon—and—*
> *Suddenly, horribly, from the sack—a baby's cry—long and loud. Jonathan starts up, gasping hugely, in horror—Dracula is right in his face:*

DRACULA:

<u>Sleep.</u>

> *The light instantly goes out. Absolute darkness. The baby's wail goes and goes and goes—and then is suddenly cut, as:*

5.

The next morning.

Jonathan, looking shaken, comes in to breakfast, at that same table. He's trying to shake off—some nightmare. A dream he can't believe. He starts, looking at Marilla and Drusilla. Drusilla, casually, is picking some...thing out of her teeth. Dracula appears behind Jonathan, making him jump:

DRACULA:
(*cheerily*) Good morning, friend Jonathan! How did you sleep?

Dracula is sounding.... more.... British?

JONATHAN:
I—beg your pardon?

DRACULA:
How. did. you. sleep?

JONATHAN:
I—(*staring at the women*) I—uh—I—

Drusilla gives a little wave. Marilla winks. Jonathan stares at them.

DRACULA:
(*snaps; does a bad impression of a hypnotist:*) Wake upppp, my Englishmunnnn!
Do sit—and let us have—a proper chat.

JONATHAN:
(*snapping out of it*) Count—
Your—your accent, sir—has it—*changed?*

DRACULA:
Why, do I sound less—(*deepening his Transylvanian accent*)

Transylvanian?
(back to British) As I said, I am making a study of you.

JONATHAN:
You are—a quick learner.

DRACULA:
You are a most enthralling subject.

> *He reaches out, as if to pick something off of his lapel—and Jonathan steps back, smiling wanly; Drusilla grins back, wolfishly.*

Were you comfortable in your room, last night?

JONATHAN:
Yes. Mhm. V-very.

DRACULA:
That is not what I have been reading.

> *He casually takes out a piece of paper—Jonathan's letter, from the night before. He reads it, doing a decent Jonathan impression, as he does.*

"Dearest Mina—On my journey here, the peasants spoke of nightmares, of atrocities and demons—and now, I find my host to be most—unnerving. I beg of you, when you receive this letter, send help as soon as you—" etcetera, etcetera.
Tsk tsk tsk tsk. This is SO HURTFUL!

> *Jonathan is very, very frightened.*

JONATHAN:
Sir—to—steal—and read a man's correspondence—is—

> *Dracula casually tears up the letter.*

DRACULA:
I would not have your wife worry for your welfare.

> *The women are advancing on him:*

JONATHAN:
Count, I—I wish to leave—you—may keep your money!

> *Now Dracula is standing—and the last thing Jonathan wants is to feel those cold hands.*

DRACULA:
—you have not yet finished my business!

JONATHAN:
> I—am troubled by strange dreams here; I am not well—

>> *Dracula's tone is so, so pleasant: he is slowly coming towards Jonathan.*

DRACULA:
> Have I not been a gracious host—as you shall be to me? Have I not treated you with courtesy?

JONATHAN:
> Yes—yes—it has been—w—wonderful—*(backing away from the women, Jonathan trips—and Dracula CATCHES him)*

DRACULA:
> *(VERY very close, and very pleasant, seductive)* Then what are you *afraid* of?

>> *Bam bam bam. Bam bam bam bam. Someone is banging on—something. The doors outside. A woman's voice; she is screaming this with grief and rage and despair:*

WOMAN (O/S):
> Demon! Devil!

DRACULA:
> *(comically)* Uh-oh.

>> *He releases Jonathan.*

WOMAN (O/S):
> Monster! Give me my child!

DRACULA:
> Welp, THIS is embarrassing.

WOMAN (O/S):
> Give me my child!

DRACULA:
> What terrible timing.

WOMAN (O/S):
> Give me my child!!!!

MARILLA:
> She sounds so miserable.

DRUSILLA:
> Let us end her pain.

Bam bam bam bam bam on the doors.

DRACULA:
No whining about your hunger tonight.

Bam bam bam bam bam; the women run out, like animals—hissing.

JONATHAN:
It was real—it—it happened—that BABY—

Bam bam BAM. Dracula is vaguely annoyed.

DRACULA:
There was a time, you know, when peasants left children at the door, as tribute. As if I were a God, or—

WOMAN (O/S):
GIVE ME MY CHILD!

DRACULA:
But the people, now, are filled with heresies—

WOMAN (O/S):
GIVE ME MY—

The bamming suddenly turns into bloodcurdling screams—which suddenly cut short—

DRACULA:
Time to move on.

He advances on Jonathan, who suddenly whips out, from his pocket, a crucifix!

JONATHAN:
Get away, you—fiend!

DRACULA:
What the—

JONATHAN:
I was given this—by my porter—there were tears in his eyes—they know what you are, I should have listened—back, monster!

Jonathan waves the crucifix at Dracula; he hisses:

I SAID BACK!

Dracula hisses, grabs the crucifix—yells in pain—pretends, as if in a bad amateur theatrical, to burn—and then casually tosses the crucifix in his hand, laughing, and drops it.

DRACULA:
What an *imagination.*

> *Jonathan stumbles back.*

I do not have *fangs.* I do not sleep in a coffin. D'you believe—if you spilled a sack of corn—I will be compelled to count every kernel?

JONATHAN:
What *are* you?

> *The women have come back in; they are drenched, DRENCHED in blood, and licking gore casually off of themselves. Again—they are animals. They watch, amused.*

DRACULA:
You are a modern fellow, Jonathan Harker, and know of Mr. Darwin's theories? I was once a man—and am now become... a superior being.

> *They circle him, rather like cats around a mouse.*

JONATHAN:
Get away!

DRACULA:
And you to me—are like the little cat to the panther.

> *Marilla reaches for him, smiling.*

> *Jonathan grabs a butter knife from the table and holds it out, trembling:*

MARILLA:
Me-ow!

> *He grabs a bigger knife.*

> *He swings towards Marilla—and Drusilla catches him easily. The women hold his arms. They are much stronger than he is. They hiss, happily. Dracula comes towards him.*

JONATHAN:
Please—I have a wife—and she is with child!

DRACULA:
—yes, the famous Mina, on holiday with her tasty schoolgirl friend.

MARILLA:
(*casually groping him*) The one who inspires such—

DRUSILLA:
(*licking his ear*) Loyalty—

DRACULA:
Aren't you tired of being a NICE man, Jonathan Harker?

MARILLA:
A meowing mewling puling weak

DRUSILLA:
Whining pleading sweet gentle little

DRACULA:
GOOD man
Don't you want to be better—

MARILLA:
Stronger—

DRUSILLA:
(*licking the side of his face*) Slicker—

DRACULA:
Don't you want to *evolve?*

> *He's so close to Jonathan now; he strokes his face—*

JONATHAN:
(*moaning as he tries to get away*) Nooo—

DRACULA:
Ladies, I think we should look in upon—these tasty British schoolchums—
And see what all the fuss is about—

JONATHAN:
Oh God, Mina—Mina!

DRACULA:
Fee fi fo fum

> *Dracula hisses, horribly, and comes into feed upon him—*

JONATHAN:
MinaaAAAAAA—AAAAA! AAAAAAA!

> *Jonathan screams.... And it echoes and echoes as we go to dark, and suddenly:*

27

6.

Britain.

Birds sing, tweet tweet; sun. A grassy, bright graveyard in the seaside town of Whitby.

Mina sits, reading over a letter. Something in it is concerning her. Next to her sits Lucy. They're both extremely bright, and have a teasing, close-knit relationship—riddled with irony and fake abuse. They're more like sisters than friends. Mina is now visibly pregnant.

LUCY:
(*she's been saying this for sometime*) Mina!

MINA:
(*coming out of her reverie*)—yes?

LUCY:
I asked how Jonathan is faring in Germania, or whathaveyou.

MINA:
You know it's Transylvania, Lucy.
Do not pretend to be stupid, to charm me. I am not your fiancé.

LUCY:
Ouch!!!

MINA:
Sorry. It's this letter.
"Dearest Mina. Transylvania is fine; I am fine; everything is fine.
Best, Jonathan Harker.
P.S. The Count is very handsome and charming."
—And he hasn't written as he said he would, this is the first I've had!

LUCY:
    Hnh. *(teasing)* Probably he's found himself some Bavarian hausfrau. Some Slovakian slattern. Some Czech chippy.

MINA:
    Ha ha.

LUCY:
    I cannot blame him, Mina. *(poking at her pregnant belly)* You have gone rather to seed.

MINA:
    That's the baby, you cow.

LUCY:
    Excuses, excuses.

MINA:
    I'll remind you how amusing that is when you are in the same condition.

LUCY:
    One step at a time, please.

MINA:
    —it happens faster than you think. One day, you're a schoolgirl, the next—

LUCY:
    a hideous bloated old broodmare—

MINA:
    —condemned to a life with no greater excitement than visiting a horrible little trollop on the seaside!

    She swats at her.

LUCY:
    Ow—*(Mina really gets her)* OW, no! Truce!

MINA:
    Brat.

LUCY:
    You can't really be concerned about him, dearest?

    Mina smoothes out the letter.

MINA:

—I know I am a married lady now, and must resign myself to no more adventures, but I should still like to experience the world—and Jonathan is my only opportunity.

LUCY:

—Is wedded life really so dull, Mina?

MINA:

—There are many rewards.

LUCY:

Of which we see evidence here. *(she pats Mina's stomach)*

MINA:

Why do you ask? *(carefully)* Do you fear—you have not chosen well in Doctor Seward?

LUCY:

Oh! No! George is so—clever, and civil, and—stable. Why???—Do you not think I have chosen well?

MINA:

His profession is—unusual. Head physician of a lunatic asylum!

LUCY:

But the world is full of madness, you know, so he shall always make an excellent living!

I just—a man may be lovely during courtship, when they are trying to win you, and then turn. It happens—all the time.

MINA:

Jonathan didn't.

LUCY:

YOU may have been fortunate, but I cannot help but be wary! I have no family, and while I am comfortable enough—without a husband, I have no standing, no prospects; I cannot even dictate how my money is spent, it's all held in trust. But our whole destinies are wrapped up in men; once we are wed we are—little better than their chattel, according to the law, and I just—wish I could be absolutely sure of his character.

    Beat.

MINA:

Dearest, if you have serious doubts about Dr. Seward—

LUCY:
>—Oh no. No. I'm being foolish. George is—the most considerate man alive.

MINA:
>Really?

LUCY:
>Yes. He takes such care of his patients, you know; worries over each one of them—just as if they were his children!

MINA:
>*Really?*

LUCY:
>YES! Don't pick at me, just because I have—bridal anxieties. You had enough before marrying Jonathan!

MINA:
>Jonathan does not run an asylum.

LUCY:
>A very KIND asylum, in which desperate cases are addressed with—with cutting-edge care! No mercury pills or lobotomies or uterus removals or anything!

MINA:
>Oh, *God.*

LUCY:
>I can prove it to you—George shall give us a tour!

MINA:
>A tour?

LUCY:
>They do them all the time, it's part of the trade!

MINA:
>An afternoon in a madhouse—what a terribly soothing prospect.

LUCY:
>Ha ha ha. Come, you judgmental shrew—*(she pulls her up; Mina swats at her)* we should go back to the house. I think a storm is coming in.

>>*Mina looks up; it is very, very dark off the coast. Somewhere, Renfield has begun praying and pacing.*

MINA:
—Heavens—that looks—quite something.

> *They both look at the clouds gathering for a moment; Renfield is praying under, her mad prayer, and it grows louder and louder as—*

LUCY:
Mm.

MINA:
—that wind! *(she shivers and pulls her shawl around her; Lucy is still staring; Mina babbles to herself)* This child, I swear it steals the heat from my bones, I am always cold and always hungry and always ready to vom-i—*(she notices Lucy's reverie)*
Lucy?
Lucy! *(she snaps in front of her face; Lucy instantly refocuses)*

LUCY:
Forgive me. I was—I was—I don't know.
Let's get you stabled, you ox. *(Mina swats her)* Ow!

> *They begin to exit; the wind is really picking up—Lucy looks at the storm again.*

MINA:
Lucy!

> *They exit—and off where Lucy was looking, a darkness is growing, growing—the wind grows louder and louder—a big crack of thunder—All goes dark—a storm is building—building—building. Wind is starting to shriek—and rain, and we see a terrible shadow of a big man—and behind him, shapes moving, and in the wind, Renfield's mad laugh—a flash of lightning, and Dracula smiles, terribly, in the white light. Blood trickles from his mouth. In Dr. Seward's Asylum, Renfield is very happy, throwing herself against the bars, dancing:*

RENFIELD:
Father!
Father, I am here
And I am ready to tattle!

> *THE LIGHTS GO OUT.*

7.

The asylum. A jingle of keys—Renfield retreats to a far wall, where she lovingly puts her hand on the prayer she scribbled; she repeats it under her breath. Doctor Seward comes in, leading Mina and Lucy on a tour—an attendant—Miller—has the keys, and has let them in.

SEWARD:
Thank you, Miller. Now—ladies—come this way, and you'll see a most interesting case.

RENFIELD:
—Our Father
Who art in Earth
Of Earth
And by Earth
Hallowed be Thy Name

She continues whispering the whole prayer under, as they continue:

MINA:
Why is this patient kept in isolation, Dr. Seward?

SEWARD:
Renfield can be—changeable. But you are very safe with me.

RENFIELD:
HA! Hahahahahaha!

SEWARD:
Lucy, dearest—you are not too frightened, are you?

LUCY:
Not with you here, George. *(she gives his arm a squeeze)* May I sit?

Seward lays down his coat for her.

MINA:
Are you all right, Lucy?

LUCY:
Only a little tired. Do go on, darling, I'm sure this case is—fascinating. *(kittenish)* I only hope I can understand it.

> *Mina rolls her eyes a little at that, but Seward preens.*

SEWARD:
I will explain it to you ladies, in the simplest terms possible.

> *He kisses her; Lucy sits out of the way; she is pale and tired.*

MINA:
Ugh.

> *Lucy hits her a little.*

SEWARD:
(performative) How is our patient today?

MILLER:
Excitable, Doctor Seward. When that big storm hit two nights ago, she was sniffing and pacing and howling, like—a dog does, when called to hunt.
And when I asked her what all the fuss was, she said: "I won't talk to you: you don't matter, for My Father is at hand." How do you like them airs?

SEWARD:
Unladylike of you, Renfield, to speak to Miller so!

RENFIELD:
Wait 'til my Father comes, *Miller*. He'll give you something to complain about.

SEWARD:	**RENFIELD:**
(gesturing to the poem, scrawled on the wall) And what is this?— I am disappointed to see this sort of behavior, again.	*(under)* Our Father Who art in Earth

SEWARD:
(he gestures towards the anti-prayer) How did she come to be able to write, I told you to take away any implements.

RENFIELD:
(under) Of Earth
And by Earth
Hallowed be Thy
Name—

MILLER:
We searched for
the chalk, sir, but
we can't find it.

SEWARD:
Such stimulation is bad for her condition. Renfield! Now where have you put that chalk?

RENFIELD:
You shall not see what my Father wills to be hidden!

SEWARD:
Be cooperative, Madame. *(getting very close)* You don't wish to lose your sugar privileges, do you?

RENFIELD:
—Pft. Always playing good Doctor, bad Doctor. Goodbadbadgood Seward.

She goes and gets the chalk from a hidden place, perhaps down her pants; as she does.

I shan't be here much longer, anyhow.

She gives it to him and sulks, stroking her poems. She sticks out her tongue at Miller; Mina is looking at Renfield, rather interested.

SEWARD:
Mrs. Renfield was once—a lady-poet—wrote wholesome verse about flowers, and the countryside, and all that.

RENFIELD:
"Roses are red, violets are blue
Renfield's a hack, who wrote lovesick goo"

SEWARD:
She went on a trip abroad—

RENFIELD:
Huzzah!

SEWARD:
—with her husband at the time—

RENFIELD:
booooo—

SEWARD:
—and was found months later, wandering on the street—like this. Come see.

LUCY:
(to Mina) Go, go. I'm fine!

RENFIELD:
I started spreading the fiery word
Preaching the gospel of rage
Instead of writing cheerful lies
And look!
They built up these
Bars and bars and bars—
And behind them, no world.

SEWARD:
Nobody has been able to find out what happened to the husband.

As if he is speaking to a child.

But we hope to make progress on that, don't we, Mrs. Renfield!

RENFIELD:
(sing songy) You shall not see what my Father wishes to remain hidden!

SEWARD:
She presents with unusual symptoms—religious—or anti-religious fervor; strong father fixation—

RENFIELD:
My Father who art in Earth—

SEWARD:
—paranoia; hysteria, of course; and, interestingly; zoophagous compulsion.

MINA:
Zoophagous?

SEWARD:
"Life-eating."
I do not mean to shock you, Mrs. Harker—but this sugar is to catch flies, which Renfield likes to swallow whole.

MINA:
Ugh!

RENFIELD:
No no NO, Doctor, that is not true—I am grown beyond such disgusting habits!

SEWARD:
—I am pleased to hear it, Renfield!

RENFIELD:
(*with great dignity*) I am graduated to spiders, and use the flies for bait.

SEWARD:
Ah. And how do they taste?

Renfield retches evocatively.

SEWARD:
You must *elect* to stop, if you do not like it. That is your homework, to exercise restraint.

RENFIELD:
(*whining*) But I need the practice.

SEWARD:
(*to Mina*) It is important—therapeutically—that she have the illusion of Choice.

RENFIELD:
Doctor—if I obey your *rules*—and do your *assignments* faithfully—may I have a kitten?

SEWARD:
A kitten?

RENFIELD:
Just one fuzzy wuzzy kitten to hold and to pet. One plump, juicy, crunchy little kitten....

MINA:
Oh, *God*.

SEWARD:
Renfield. Do stop, you are causing Mrs. Harker distress.

MINA:
Are you SURE she isn't dangerous?

SEWARD:
Not if I'm here.

RENFIELD:
Hahahahaha!

MINA:
What is she laughing at?

SEWARD:
It is really impossible to /say—

RENFIELD:
/I am laughing at YOU, Seward.
"Not if I'm here, you'll be safe with me."

> *She swivels, her strange eyes finally on Mina.*

Hello little mother.
Do you like my poem?

MINA:
It is... interesting.

RENFIELD:
Won't you close your eyes, and let me read it to you?

MINA:
No—thank you.

RENFIELD:
Can I tell you a secret? *(she beckons—Mina gets closer; Renfield starts in a half-whisper)* It feels nice to let go and listen in the dark—
you should TRY IT—

> *Suddenly frantic; Renfield tries to grab her arm; Mina jerks back.*

SEWARD:
Renfield! No touching!

RENFIELD:
Do not let the goodbad doctor deceive you!!!
Do not put your faith in your husband!

MINA:
The—the doctor is not my husband.

RENFIELD:
You wear a ring, as I once did—like a manacle.

MINA:
My husband is abroad.

RENFIELD:
>Do not trust *him*, either!
>Any of them!
>As long as they have power over us
>They shall always abuse it!

SEWARD:
>Renfield—this is nonsense.

RENFIELD:
>Your man can lock you away for being mad, you know
>They say what madness is!
>They define all the words!
>They make all the rules—
>And they don't let you break them
>And they try to break you if you try!
>Once you belong to him—
>He may dispose of you how he will
>And you may scream and scream
>And never be heard!

MINA:
>Is that true, Doctor Seward? Can a woman be—shut away just because her husband claims she is mad?

SEWARD:
>...—that is a terrible abuse of the system, and certainly not true in this case, since nobody has seen Mr. Renfield since—

RENFIELD:
>Since I was delivered!
>I had faith in their authority once
>Worshipped the shibboleth of chivalry
>Sold my soul for sweet words—
>And only my Father freed me
>From the tyranny of
>The *bad* man, my *husband*.
>I do not know why my Savior wills now
>That I should be locked away.
>But I shall prove my worth—
>And have my reward!
>And then He shall give me
>Strength beyond measure!
>What bars will hold me then?
>Watch out, Doctor.
>Daddy is coming!

MILLER:
Doctor Seward—Miss Westenra—!

Lucy is slumped over, seemingly in a faint.

RENFIELD:
Miss is better than Mrs.!

SEWARD:
Lucy!

MINA:
—are you all right?

RENFIELD:
(Finally spotting Lucy) Oh—!

LUCY:
—I just—got dizzy—

Renfield prostrates herself:

RENFIELD:
Forgive me, my Lady,
I should not have prattled bad poetry to Naughty children!
I did not know you were here,
I would have composed odes to your beauty—

Renfield is frantic; Lucy is trying to get out.

LUCY:
Why is she speaking to me in that way?

SEWARD:
She is—delusional, darling, I wouldn't be /concerned—

RENFIELD:
/You will tell my Father I spread his word, won't you?

LUCY:
(upset) Take me out, George?

RENFIELD:
Tell Him that I keep the faith!

SEWARD:
—I should not have brought you here—

He leads Lucy out—

Miller—restrain Renfield before she hurts herself.

RENFIELD:

—NO! NO! NO! NOOOOOOOOO!

> *Miller restrains Renfield; she screams miserably as she is pinned down—Mina is torn between concern for Lucy and horror at Renfield's rough treatment. Renfield screams until Miller gags her.*

MINA:

Don't—don't hurt her.

> *Renfield whimpers—Miller cuffs her.*

MILLER:

Wouldn't waste sympathy on this one, Miss, just because she talks philosophical rubbish.

> *Renfield gives something like a growl.*

Thing that gotten her locked away, was bad enough.

MINA:

—what did she do?

MILLER:

She attacked a baby. And if the mother hadn't fought her off in time—*(Renfield snaps at her; she cuffs her again)* Eh eh eh! No biting.

> *Renfield's strange mad eyes land on Mina, she whines, very like an animal. Mina backs away, horrified, as we transition to:*

8.

Lucy's bed chamber. She is sitting up, resting.

SEWARD:
Feeling any better?

LUCY:
You were right, George—it was only a moment's weakness. Why are you always so clever?

Mina rolls her eyes, coughs.

SEWARD:
I should not have brought you today, Lucy, it was—too shocking for a lady's sensibilities.

Mina coughs again, aggrieved.

SEWARD:
(*still focused on Lucy*) You'll need to refrain from stimulation for a few days.

LUCY:
Then I shall have to stay away from *you*, George.

Mina coughs, appalled.

SEWARD:
I'll be back in the morning.

LUCY:
I'll miss you so.

Mina makes something very like a RETCHING sound. Seward exits; Lucy holds the pose—and then breaks it as soon as he disappears. She throws a pillow at Mina.

LUCY:
Are you quite done?

MINA:
Really, Lucy. *"Why are you always so clever? Then I shall have to stay away from you, George,"* batting your lashes and dumbing yourself down and playing the fantasy, every moment.
Small wonder you are feeling ill!

LUCY:
Oh, Mina, hush! Simple for you to say, you are married already. I must ease my way into—

MINA:
Into ever being genuine?

LUCY:
Men play their roles, we play ours. Who knows what's underneath?

MINA:
You risk a lifetime of unhappiness—if you always suspect him, and conceal your self.

LUCY:
Stop.

MINA:	**LUCY:**
/I'm just	/Stop, stop, lalala I can't hear you. /*(kittenish)* Be nice to me, I'm sick!

MINA:
—Do you think this sudden weakness is a manifestation of "bridal anxieties?"

LUCY:
I don't— I have not been sleeping well, the last few nights. And today—that woman—

Beat—Mina rubs her back.

How—terrifying—that men can lock us away, if we run too wild.

MINA:
—Mrs. Renfield is a rather extreme case.

LUCY:
Still. It is awful to think—that I am putting myself under someone's power, so completely.

MINA:
You do have some say in the matter.

LUCY:
Yes, *(with some bitterness)* "It is important—therapeutically—that she have the illusion of choice."

> *Somewhere, a clock chimes: it is just past 10.*

MINA:
I should go to my room.

LUCY:
(she grabs Mina's hand, for a moment) I just wish—that we didn't have to become respectable ladies and find husbands and give up all of our adventures! That we—could stay mad young creatures—forever.

> *Mina kisses her forehead and smoothes her covers.*

MINA:
Close your eyes, dearest. Drift off.
There must be some alternative.

> *Mina begins to exit, caressing her stomach.*

There must be.

> *She blows out the candle. The lights go black.*

> *Far away church bells strike midnight, There is a susurration—as if of wings and in the blackness, we hear a refrain:*

RENFIELD:
Once you belong to him—
He may dispose of you how he will
And you may scream and scream
And never be heard!
Hahahaha!

> *Lucy gasps, hugely—and all goes black.*

9.

Mina enters, drawing the curtain.

MINA:
Good morning, you horrible little monster! How did you sleep?

LUCY:
Mm—

MINA:
—Lucy? How did you sleep?

> *She puts a hand to Lucy's shoulder:*

LUCY:
(half out of consciousness, as if in a dream)
No no—no—no—no—no

> *She is terribly pale; looks sick; she starts—moaning—screaming and thrashing—as if trying to come out of a nightmare; and then seizes violently.*

MINA:
Help! HELP! SOMEBODY HELP!

10.

Lucy thrashes, her eyes rolling back into her head. Dr. Seward rushes in and bends over Mina sits with her, frightened. A maid hovers.

SEWARD:
Dehydration, hallucinations. Mild abrasions—but no fever, no signs of infection.

MINA:
What—what can it be?

SEWARD:
I don't know.

MINA:
What are you going to do?!!

SEWARD:
None of this makes any sense!

MINA:
Seward—

He doesn't answer.

Can—can—*I* do anything to help—at all—there must be something—

SEWARD:
Mrs. Harker—just—shush! I am trying to think!

MINA:
"Shush?"

SEWARD:

There is a specialist on the London lecture circuit, at the moment; a Doctor Van Helsing, who makes a study of strange diseases. I have never met the man, but I have read his work—he may have some theories—

MINA:

Send to him at once!

SEWARD:

—yes, yes. OBVIOUSLY—*(he begins scrawling something down on a sheet of paper)*

Lucy moans, terribly, shudders and is still; they both pause, troubled.

MINA:

I will stay with her tonight.

SEWARD:

(still scrawling)—that is not advisable—in your condition.

MINA:

—I am fine.

SEWARD:

Your husband would insist.

MINA:

My husband is not here!!! And I am still—perfectly capable of being useful!

SEWARD:

I appreciate your concern, Mrs. Harker, but indulging in hysterics will not help!

MINA:

Hysterics?

The maid has entered and awkwardly caught the last of that.

MAID:

Letter for you, Ma'am.

SEWARD:

She sleeps alone tonight. Doctor's orders.

Mina opens the letter—whatever it is really irritates her. The maid and Seward exit as he beckons for her re: the note. Mina reads from the letter:

MINA:
"Charming Mina,
I am delayed in my return. But do not worry. I am better than ever...
Jonathan Harker
P.S. The Count is a most gracious host."

(Mina angrily crumples the letter, throws it away)

"Doctor's orders."

(She defiantly climbs into bed with Lucy.)

11.

> *The lights go out. The clock strikes midnight—and we hear the same soft susurration. Mina has fallen asleep. But this time—it's not totally dark. Perhaps a strange light comes on—a sick, sallow light, as if reality has suspended. Lucy whimpers, softly, and thrashes a little:*

DRUSILLA:
Come, sister—

MARILLA:
Come sister—*(Lucy's eyes pop open.)*

> *Lucy, carefully, as in a dream, gets out of bed. From—somewhere—now very close—we hear those whispers:*

DRUSILLA:
Don't you wish—

MARILLA:
To feel powerful—
Don't you want—

DRUSILLA:
To be strong—
Don't you yearn—

MARILLA:
To live free?

> *Lucy has picked her way across the floor—*

DRUSILLA AND MARILLA:
Let us in.

> *Lucy opens the window. From the dark, Marilla and Drusilla appear—*

DRUSILLA:
D'awww— the poor naive young things

MARILLA:
Sweet benighted girls—

DRUSILLA:
Time after time:

MARILLA:
Year after year—

DRUSILLA:
Falling for easy promises.

MARILLA:
Shall we never learn.

> *Marilla violently clamps her hand over Lucy's mouth: Drusilla holds her back—and Dracula is in the room. Lucy is, suddenly, conscious.*

DRACULA:
Lovely Lucy Westenra.
What a pleasure to see you again.
Remember last night's adventures, beauty?
Shall I remind you?

> *He bares his teeth—hisses, and comes in to feed; Lucy gives a little cry—and Mina wakes up.*

MINA:
Lucy?!!

> *She lights the candle—and suddenly sees them; it's a nightmare.*

DRACULA:
The famous Mrs. Harker!

> *She scrabbles up.*

MINA:
(*soundless—so, so terrified*) (—Oh my—)

DRACULA:
You—are not quite my taste.

> *Mina draws breath to scream:*

<u>Sleep.</u>

> *Everything goes black as Mina falls back into the bed. A beat. Two.*

12.

In the dark, we suddenly hear—SCREAMING, SCREAMING—and Mina starts awake—the lights come on as she does—the maid is screaming. In the bed, lies Lucy. All down the front of her dress—all over her mouth—is blood. Lucy twitches—as if thrashing against unseen hands. The blood is over everything—smearing, smearing the white sheets... Mina starts back. The maid runs for help.

MINA:
Lucy?!! oh my God—

LUCY:
(gasping) Mina—
Thought—my— choice—
Stupid girl—

MINA:
Lucy!

Lucy starts screaming—then thrashes and thrashes, and LAUGHS, horribly—it hurts her. Seward runs in and restrains her—and her screams subside to moans...She is gasping—gasping—gasping for air—and then she is silent—still covered in blood... still seizing and twitching, as if fighting in a dream.

13.

Later.

SEWARD:
I've given her laudanum. That should calm her.

MINA:
What is happening to her?

SEWARD:
You tell me! You were here!!

MINA:
Yes—but, I just slept! I had—nightmares, but—that's it!

SEWARD:
Oh, nightmares! Fat lot of good information, there! Well-done, you!!!

MINA:
I beg your pardon?!!

SEWARD:
I told you not to stay with her, didn't I?!!

MINA:
You cannot be saying that this is my fault?!

SEWARD:
You did not listen to my orders. And now she is worse than ever!

>*Lucy moans again as if in a nightmare, pants very hard like she's panicking—thrashes.*

SEWARD:
Lucy? I'm here. *(he holds her to stop her from thrashing)* Lucy—darling—it's George.

Then suddenly—Lucy's eyes fly open. She goes totally still—she smiles; she's calm. And her voice is—different. Very like Marilla and Drusilla's predator drawl.

LUCY:
Oh, *George.*
Hello.
How s*weet* of you, to attend upon me.

MINA:
Lucy?

LUCY:
Visiting me in bed. So *naughty.* And here I thought you were such a *nice* boy.
Won't you kiss me, my love.

SEWARD:
(very conscious of Mina right there; Lucy is entwining around him) Oh—um—Lucy—this is—you are not well—

LUCY:
I have never been better

SEWARD:
Ouch!

LUCY:
—Mmmmm—

MINA:
Seward, she is—not herself—

SEWARD:
Mania may be—a side effect of—*(she grabs something sensitive)*—LUCY!

LUCY:
You know you want to—

SEWARD:
I ah—I, oh, heavens, that's—

LUCY:
Give it up now. Give in, give it.

SEWARD:
Well—all right—

She nuzzles him, then begins to pull him in—are her teeth—gleaming?

VAN HELSING:
STOP.

>   *Van Helsing has arrived. Lucy gives something like a half-snarl, half sulky-drugged pout; she slumps back when Seward disentangles himself. She falls back into unconsciousness.*

I wouldn't do that, if I were you.

SEWARD:
Who are you?!

14.

Van Helsing is a woman. Not only that, she's a woman in a cowboy hat. She's American. She wears dusty beaten clothing and a big cowboy hat. She has one, long nasty old scar all up and down the side of her face.

VAN HELSING:
I—am Dr. Van Helsing.

SEWARD:
You?

VAN HELSING:
—what, you were expecting a withered old Dutch man?

SEWARD:
But—you're a woman!

VAN HELSING:
You noticed.

SEWARD:
And you are—you can't be—a doctor?

VAN HELSING:
—There are a few universities, now, that admit women.

SEWARD:
For a *fee*, yes.

VAN HELSING:
And who you are, exactly?

SEWARD:
I am—Doctor Seward.

VAN HELSING:
Seward. Got your letter. Came to help. *(she holds out her hand to shake)*

SEWARD:
But—

VAN HELSING:
You're welcome.

SEWARD:
But—

VAN HELSING:
(she drops her hand, and strides past him) Hold my hat.

She thrusts her hat at him.

SEWARD:
But—! *(he's left holding the hat)*

MINA:
Doctor Van Helsing—This is Lucy Westenra.

VAN HELSING:
(kindly, as she examines) Hello, little one. Not feeling well, are we?

Lucy moans and gives a little snarl.

—What have you been giving her?

SEWARD:
I—opiates—to calm her.

VAN HELSING:
Opiates to make her muddled and tractable—incapable of resistance.
Stupid choice.

SEWARD:
EXCUSE ME, Madame—

VAN HELSING:
Doctor.
(to Mina) Has Miss Westenra said anything of note?

SEWARD:
Only... babbling; she's been hallucinating—

VAN HELSING:
What exactly did she say?

SEWARD:
Nonsense, rubbish, I don't know—I was not marking it.

VAN HELSING:
Typical.

MINA:
She said—she said it was her choice.

VAN HELSING:
Huh. *(she looks at Mina)* Well.—SOMEBODY was listening to Miss Westenra.

MINA:
—I slept alongside her last night.

VAN HELSING:
And how did you sleep?

SEWARD:
Why are /you—

VAN HELSING:
/Let her speak.

MINA:
—I had—nightmares?

VAN HELSING:
I bet you did. Can you remember any specifics?

SEWARD:
I wrote to you to consult on Lucy's treatment, not—analyze dreams, Madame!

VAN HELSING:
Doctor.

> *She gestures back to Mina.*

MINA:
No specifics—I'm sorry, it's all—cloudy.

VAN HELSING:
If anything comes back, tell me.
(examining Lucy) Now—let's take a closer look—

SEWARD:
I must insist—

VAN HELSING:
Shush, Seward! Let me work.

SEWARD:
"Shush?"

VAN HELSING:
You—*(to Mina)* help me turn her.

MINA:
Me?

VAN HELSING:
Why not you?

SEWARD:
(to Van Helsing) What—what can I do?

VAN HELSING:
You—can fetch me a coffee.

> *She begins examining Lucy, peering at her mouth; to Mina:*

Mind your fingers—don't get near her mouth.

SEWARD:
(hovering) Have you ever seen anything like this before? *(Van Helsing ignores him, keeps examining)*
Van Helsing? Do you have any theories about the nature of this disease?

VAN HELSING:
(upon looking in Lucy's mouth) So I thought.

SEWARD:
Van Helsing?!! Do you know what this disease is?!!!

VAN HELSING:
Poor child.

> *Van Helsing strides back to the bag—and begins taking out a simple device—as she does, and she ignores him, going spontaneously deaf.*

SEWARD:
VAN HELSING!!!! HELLO?!! HELLO?!!! **HELLO?!!!! WHAT IS THIS DISEASE?!!**

VAN HELSING:
(turning, calmly, in his face)—Sit. *(he jumps back)*

SEWARD:
(thinking it's the name of a disease) What is "SIT"?!

VAN HELSING:
Sit... *(he still stares at her)* As in put—your butt, down, on the chair, and roll back your sleeve. I'm giving her a blood transfusion.

SEWARD:
What—why—I insist that you explain, Madame!

VAN HELSING:
Doctor. And I insist that I show you in practice! Sit!

SEWARD:
You cannot just come in here and—and take over—I must be—consulted! It is my right!

MINA:
Doctor Seward is also Lucy's fiancé, Doctor Van Helsing.

VAN HELSING:
Congratulations.
—Your fiancé is dying, Seward—

MINA:
Dying?

VAN HELSING:
—and you will not save her by grandstanding! SIT!

SEWARD:
(he will not sit) I—I—this is really—

MINA:
Oh for God's sake, *I'll* do it!

She sits, quickly.

VAN HELSING:
—What is your name, again?

SEWARD:
This is Mrs. Jonathan Harker—

VAN HELSING:
She may talk for herself. What is your name?

MINA:
Mina. Mrs. Mina Harker. And I'll give, to save Lucy.

SEWARD:
That is not advisable, Mrs. Harker, in your condition!

VAN HELSING:
STOP SPEAKING FOR HER!
—He's right—for once. This is draining work—ha ha—and not good for the baby. But you, Seward, you're a big strong man. Be half as brave as Mina Harker.

> *She kicks him the stool. Seward sits, reluctantly, and Van Helsing instantly stabs him with the needle.*

MINA:
Can't I do—anything?

VAN HELSING:
Go to the market—get me as many garlic bulbs as you can find.

SEWARD:
What are you—making soup?

VAN HELSING:
Seward, you are as talented a comedian as you are a doctor.

SEWARD:
Why would you need—

VAN HELSING:
Shush, man, *(lying)* talking will make you light-headed.

> *She slaps his back in a friendly way—too hard. To Mina:*

Garlic!

> *Seward yelps, a high girlish yelp. As the blood reaches Lucy, she finds a little comfort—breathes, and settles; Van Helsing feels her forehead.*

15.

Mina visits a stall, in the marketplace.

MINA:
Every bulb you have.

MERCHANT:
—you must be making some recipe, Missus.

MINA:
I don't know *what* I'm doing.

> *Someone is coming—dirty and shambling, wrapped up in rags—babbling, very fast.*

JONATHAN:	**MERCHANT:**
—It was late at night so late and so dark—	Oh, no.

> *The Merchant hurries out to intercept the figure; she may have a broom.*

JONATHAN:	**MERCHANT:**
It's not s*cary*, it's not— It doesn't feel *bad*, you don't— Have to worry,	No, no, no—none of that here—off! Begone!

MERCHANT:
Damned crazy vagrants make nuisances of themselves / and the city won't do a thing—

JONATHAN:
/All prophets are thought mad in their day!

MINA:
Jonathan?

JONATHAN:
So laugh if you want,
You bad brats!
Turn up your noses!

MERCHANT:
always the same rant—
I've told you a dozen
times—out!

MINA:
Jonathan!!!!!

Jonathan finally stops, and peers at her—

What are you doing here?!!!

JONATHAN:
I—what am I—doing—

MINA:
Why are you so dirty and— you *smell* like—

MERCHANT:
Do you *know* this fellow, Missus?

MINA:
—this is my husband!

MERCHANT:
(*Jonathan is poking random things*) He's been around for weeks—stealing food—And raving! About—wild things!

JONATHAN:
(*peering at Mina*) Who are you?

MINA:
Jonathan—it's—it's Mina.

She touches his arm; he peers at her.

JONATHAN:
Mi—Mina—oh God, Mina—I—had to escape, I—have to get away, I—

He suddenly falls down starts convulsing, seizing, as if reliving something.

MINA:
Jonathan!

JONATHAN:
He is—coming—he—is—come
No, no! No!

Jonathan shakes and seizes; Mina tries to hold him down.

MERCHANT:
So... should I still wrap these up for you, or—?
Right.

16.

Jonathan is lifted up and carried into a bed, where he tosses and turns—then tenses—and suddenly lies still. Mina waits with him, anxious. The doctor's back is to us as he bends over Jonathan. He holds a finger—"hush"—to Mina, who looks upset. Then he leaves. <u>The doctor is played by the same actor as Dracula.</u>

MAID:
What happened to him, Ma'am.

MINA:
The doctor says—a brain fever; that he's had some kind of—terrible shock. And that—I must not ask him upsetting questions, or I may—provoke his fits again.

MAID:
(crossing herself fearfully) He's gone mad—just like Miss Lucy.

MINA:
DON'T say that. He's not—he's not as ill as Lucy, his pulse is very strong—and his lucidity should return once we treat his body.

MAID:
What if it don't?

>Beat.

MINA:
—he should sleep now. When he wakes—we'll have to give him broths, that kind of thing.

MAID:
There's already one invalid in this house—staff is stretched thin as it is!

MINA:
There is nothing to be done for it but broths.

MAID:
—don't get paid enough for this.

MINA:
(losing it) BROTHS.

> *The maid exits. Mina crawls into bed with Jonathan, strokes his face. He is still.*

17.

Lucy's bedchamber. Garlic flowers and bulbs hung all around it. Van Helsing works on a wreath of garlic flowers. Seward is rubbing his arm—he looks weak and pale.

MAID:
Oh, Doctor—Miss Westenra looks so much improved!

VAN HELSING:
I know.

MAID:
You're some kind of a—genius!

VAN HELSING:
(still working on the wreath) I know.

SEWARD:
Ugh.

MAID:
You all right, sir?

SEWARD:
Yes—

VAN HELSING:
No—I took two pints from him—he should rest, as I have told him again and again—

SEWARD:
God, I hate a lecture—

VAN HELSING:
—but the fool will not listen!

SEWARD:
My place is here. And you gave, too!

VAN HELSING:
Yes, but I am—(*giving a tug to the knot of the wreath*)—reMARKably strong.

> *She grins. Van Helsing and Steward really push each other's buttons.*

SEWARD:
Is that how you got that scar, Van Helsing? One too many boasts?

> *She snorts, and does not reply. She gently puts the garlic wreath around Lucy's neck.*

SEWARD:
What is that for?

VAN HELSING:
(*evading the question*) Folk medicine. Garlic has healing properties.

SEWARD:
The room stinks of it!

VAN HELSING:
Better safe than sorry.

> *Van Helsing has taken a little silver necklace from her own neck—a small crucifix—and put it around Lucy's neck.*

SEWARD:
—all right, now what is THAT for?

VAN HELSING:
—let's say luck.

> *Lucy is struggling a bit, reaching towards it.*

SEWARD:
It bothers her—she is scratching at it!

> *He reaches to remove it; she stops him.*

VAN HELSING:
Don't! (*he reaches for it again*)
I said, DON'T!
Didn't the transfusion work?! Isn't she improved?!

SEWARD:
Yes—

VAN HELSING:
Then stop questioning my methods!

SEWARD:
Not until you tell me what the—the h-e-l-l is going on!

VAN HELSING:
H-e-?

SEWARD:
I will not curse in front of a lady!

VAN HELSING:
I am no Lady. But I am a medical professional!

SEWARD:
I am ALSO a professional, and you have no right to exclude me! Blood transfusion—that has a rational basis. And I concede that she is better!

VAN HELSING:
—good of you./

SEWARD:
/But what does that have to do with—with garlic on the sill, or silver crosses or—dancing around toadstools under a full moon, or whatever you are about to propose?
You still will not tell me what this dis-ease is!

VAN HELSING:
You're not ready to hear it.

SEWARD:
I am a modern man, I am a man of science, I am perfectly open-minded.

VAN HELSING:
You seem to me, Seward—to be someone who believes only in his own senses. But you must trust, that I know firsthand what I speak of, even if it is—outside the realm of your known experience. (*she takes a deep breath, then:*) I believe your fiancé is under the control of a supernatural creature.

SEWARD:
Excuse me?

VAN HELSING:
/ *Das Wampir* in German, *vetalas* in Sanskrit; *izcackus* in Hungarian.

Tales of these beings date back to the Mesopotamians—

SEWARD:
Is this a *joke*—

VAN HELSING:
Narratives vary, but there are stories from every culture—consistencies / that cannot be overlooked—

SEWARD:
/STOP! Stop! Those are OLD WIVES' TALES!

VAN HELSING:
When the ruling class write history, the words of the common people, of women—become superstition / but there is truth in—

SEWARD:
Unbelievable—

VAN HELSING:
The unbelievable quickly becomes believable—if pigheaded men will only listen!

SEWARD:
—What are you—looking for money?

Van Helsing balks.

No doubt you'll charge a hefty fee to conduct your exorcisms?!!!

VAN HELSING:
I'm warning you, Seward—

SEWARD:
No, I'm warning you. Get out of this house!
I will treat Lucy myself from now on!

VAN HELSING:
That's a mistake.

SEWARD:
This was the mistake.
You are a swindler. A hustler. A quack. And you are dismissed, Van Helsing.

VAN HELSING:
—watch over her, fool.

SEWARD:
Out!

Van Helsing exits. Seward is very, very angry.
Lucy moans, scratching at the necklace.

SEWARD:
Here, Lucy. Here, my love.

He takes off the necklace—throwing it to the side. She is still restless. He takes off the wreath of flowers, throwing it aside. Then, angry—he starts pulling down all the garlic. He opens the window. He throws the garlic out of it. Something about the air—makes him shiver. He closes and locks the window, annoyed by his own superstition. Then, he sits next to Lucy, determined, holding her hand. He settles to watch her.

18.

Dark. Mina sleeps next to Jonathan—Seward has dropped off, next to Lucy's bed.

The clock strikes midnight. Both Jonathan and Lucy's eyes snap open. Jonathan goes to the window—and opens it. He gives a sort of beckoning gesture—and a mist pours in.

The mist curls around Lucy, in her room.

JONATHAN:
Come.

MARILLA (O/S):
Come, sister

DRUSILLA (O/S):
Come, sister.

(Jonathan goes back to bed. Lucy silently gets up from the bed. She walks out of the room—just as she passes, Jonathan rolls over to Mina. He begins to hug her—closer and closer, keeping her pinned down. She wakes up:)

MINA:
Jonathan—darling.
....You're hurting me!
Stop—!
Help! Help! HELP!

The maid runs in, in her nightgown.

MINA:
JONATHAN!

She finally slaps him, hard.

JONATHAN;

—He is—come.

He slumps and passes out.

MAID:

—You all right, Miss?

MINA:

No! He had some kind of a—fit!

MAID:

(poking at Jonathan experimentally) Thought the Doctor poured laudanum into him—where did he get the strength?

MINA:

(losing it) And why is it is—FOGGY in here, *(she waves the mist away)* where did this come from, it's like a nightmare—

MAID:

Oh—*(she screams a little)* Miss—there's a figure, out there on the street.

MINA:

(she runs to the window) It's—it's Lucy!

MAID:

What?

MINA:

(calling out) Lucy!

Mina whips on a shawl and goes running out.

JONATHAN:

(moaning, his eyes closed) He—is come.

Jonathan shudders and is still.

MAID:

—don't get paid enough for this.

We VERY QUICKLY transition to: the graveyard.

19.

> *Lucy comes in—still in that dreamlike state. They wait for her.*

MARILLA:
　Come, sister

DRUSILLA:
　Come, sister—

MARILLA:
　Come where you will always be wild

MINA (O/S):
　Lucy!

DRUSILLA:
　Come where you will always be full

MARILLA:
　Come where you will always be free

MINA (O/S):
　Lucy!

MARILLA AND DRUSILLA:
　Come—

> *Lucy is left, swaying, before Dracula.*

DRACULA:
　Give it up, my beauty.
　Give in to me, my sweet.
　Give and you shall receive.

> *Mina has stumbled up, panting; she has a lantern.*

MINA:
　—LUCY!!!

She sees Dracula and gasps in horror.

DRACULA:
You again?

MINA:
You're the nightmare!

DRACULA:
(happily) Yes!

MINA:
(frantic, so loud it almost wakes her) **LUCY!**

LUCY:
M—Mina?

DRACULA:
No—no. *(snapping in Lucy's face)* quit it.
(harsh) /Shhh.

LUCY:
(falling under) Shh—shhh

DRACULA:
(never taking his eyes from Lucy, and smiling all the while)
Mina Harker, you are **decidedly**
Not my taste.
But my wives—are not so particular.

> *He snaps; the women surround Mina, circling like a pack of dogs. He hisses and begins to feed on Lucy—she chokes and starts to scream, but cannot.*

MINA:
LUCY!!!!!

DRACULA:
Drink of this blood, eat of this body
Which has been given up to you—
And all your struggles will be over.

> *Mina cannot get to Lucy—the women circle her. Lucy is on her knees now; close to death—and Dracula takes a nail and slits open a wound on his own chest, which bleeds.*

MINA:
Help! HELP!

> *Lucy, with a little moan—begins to feed. Dracula gives a little half-sexual sound. Drusilla and Marilla hiss, and surround Mina—it is just like when they surrounded Jonathan:*

DRUSILLA:
Poor little mother!
We can smell—
Your fear, darling—

MARILLA:
That *nice* man you left in your bed—

DRUSILLA:
—Even the child in your belly—

MARILLA:
And may we say they smell

DRUSILLA:
Delicious....

> *Mina opens her mouth to try to scream—but nothing comes out; Dracula moans. The women hiss and are about to feed, when:*

VAN HELSING:
BACK, MONSTERS!

> *Van Helsing has a pair of stakes, which she brandishes—the women hiss and fall back; they're almost amused.*

I SAID, BACK!

MARILLA:
Look, Drusilla! A gen-you-wine American cow-girl!

DRUSILLA:
A puffed-up country bumpkin!

MARILLA:
A clumsy wanna-be savior.

> *Van Helsing swings at them—*

VAN HELSING:
BACK!

DRUSILLA:
Would you hurt
A harmless cooing
Creature like me?

MARILLA:
Will you maim my pretty body
With your pointed sticks, Madame?

VAN HELSING:
It's "Doctor."

Mina, half-stunned, crawls behind her:

MARILLA:
Doctor? *(fake-impressed)* Ho ho ho
Aren't WE impressed

DRUSILLA:
Times do change, Marilla—

And then fast, fast—my God, so fast that you realize they've only been resting, lazily, all this time, they are darting towards them—

VAN HELSING:
BACK!

She flings a grey powder at them, and unexpectedly, both women SCREAM as they come in contact with it, and retreat instantly, as if it's burning them.

VAN HELSING:
Mina, are you all right?!!

MARILLA:
(wailing) My eyes! It's in my eyes!

MINA:
Lucy—he has Lucy!

VAN HELSING:
He?!!

DRUSILLA:
Husband!

She darts back to where Dracula is, in the shadows—and he suddenly rises up. His once pristine shirt is covered in Lucy's blood. Blood on his mouth, on his hands. And he is big—all of a sudden, he looks even bigger. It is like watching a very big wave on the ocean, getting bigger and bigger and—

VAN HELSING:
(very frightened) Oh, God.

DRACULA:
Close enough.

MARILLA:
My eyes!

DRACULA:
Burning powders, hm?
Nasty.

VAN HELSING:
I have more—tricks up my sleeve!

DRACULA:
Big declarations from
A shaking little woman.

VAN HELSING:
Get away—I'm warning you!

DRACULA:
OoOOoOO.

Half-laughing.

I met rebels in the old country—
I suppose I could not hope to escape them in the new.
Too bad, Hunter—
You come too late.

He makes a gesture and Mina's lantern goes out. It goes completely dark—and he disappears. That same susurration.

MINA:
(panicking) Oh God, Oh God—

Van Helsing lights a match—and rekindles the lantern.

Lucy!

Mina stumbles over to Lucy, who's lying on the ground.

VAN HELSING:
Careful!

MINA:
She's not breathing—Doctor Van Helsing, help her!!!

VAN HELSING:
It is too late.

She pulls Mina away from the body.

MINA:
(sobbing) —please—Lucy— it can't be over.

VAN HELSING:
—It's not.

She leads Mina away. Lucy's body is left alone in the old graveyard.

RENFIELD:
And then he shall give me strength beyond measure!
What bars will hold me then?
Watch out, Doctor!
Daddy is coming!

DRUSILLA:
Come, sister—

MARILLA:
Come, sister—

DRACULA:
Come.

Lucy's eyes snap open.

Intermission.

ACT TWO

1.

Lucy's body is laid out in her own house; she is wrapped in white linen. The blood doesn't show, and she is peaceful. Clean, clean, clean. Mina is wrapped, shivering from shock, in another white sheet. Van Helsing sits, grimly, inspecting her stakes. Seward is in shock.

MINA:
—and then the—creatures—disappeared—and—Lucy was gone.

Beat.

SEWARD:
None of this—makes any sense.
She chose, to leave me? To go to this—other man?

VAN HELSING:
Not a man. And not actually a choice.
I think she was confused, Seward. They can cloud minds—make imprisonment seem like freedom.

SEWARD:
—No.

VAN HELSING:
"No?"

SEWARD:
Lucy would never have—done that. We were—happy.

Beat.

VAN HELSING:
We can discuss it later. It's time to prepare the corpse.

SEWARD:
"Prepare the—?"

VAN HELSING:
So that infection does not spread.

> *She walks towards Lucy's body, pulling out a big nasty saw—*

SEWARD:
STOP!

> *She begins to head towards the body again.*

I said, **STOP!** Before I—I am forced to—lay hands on you!

VAN HELSING:
Try.

> *It's a face-off; Mina tries to break it up.*

MINA:
Seward, trust Doctor Van Helsing! You have no idea what you're dealing with!

> *Van Helsing goes for that saw again—heck, maybe even a bigger saw.*

SEWARD:
Van Helsing—you will have nothing to do with her body! And you *(to Mina)*—will stop spreading disgusting, salacious slander about her!

MINA:
I know what I saw!

SEWARD:
She will be laid to rest, in peace; as she lived—an angel, beyond any reproach!

MINA:
An angel?!!! Lucy was vulgar—and—and clever—and complicated—she was not some porcelain idol for you to worship! You didn't even *know* her!!

> *Beat.*

SEWARD:
Mrs. Harker. Calm down, or I shall have you removed.

MINA:
You can't do /—

SEWARD:

/I am now left to order Lucy's affairs. If you do not stop speaking *nonsense*, I can have you thrown out of this house, and your husband, too.

MINA:

You pompous, pigheaded *(she never ever swears)* ASS!

SEWARD:

You are upset—and this woman has taken advantage of your pain and shock and your condition to—to influence you. But I will not hear one more word about—supernatural creatures, or moonlit seductions, or whatever other madness this—huckster has convinced you is true!
Now, Van Helsing, shall I call for the constabulary, or will you leave like a lady?

VAN HELSING:

I am no Lady.

Seward storms out.

Van Helsing has hurried over to Lucy's body and is unwrapping a silver cross necklace from around her neck, which she quickly puts around Lucy's neck.

MINA:

Of all the closed-minded, shallow-thinking, condescending fools—

VAN HELSING:

He wants somebody to blame, besides himself.
But I only needed a moment.

MINA:

What?

VAN HELSING:

—Thank you for provoking him so thoroughly! You've got a real talent for it.

Van Helsing arranges Lucy's clothes so the little crucifix is hidden—Seward comes rushing back in, the maid behind him.

SEWARD:

I've sent for the constable! So you'd better—clear out, you!

VAN HELSING:

(She touches Lucy's hair—like a blessing) —My condolences, Seward.

She tips her hat, and exits.

SEWARD:

Mrs. Harker. They say your husband has awakened.
You should attend upon him.

MINA:

I know these are shocking times, Doctor.
(very angry and tight) But may I suggest—that you stop commanding and start *listening.*
(looking at Lucy) As you should have listened—from the beginning.

She exits. Seward watches after her, for a moment:

MAID:

(crying) Oh, poor Miss Westenra! Taken away so young!

She crosses herself and kneels by the body.

SEWARD:

Watch over her.

MAID:

(The maid begins to pray, loudly)
Our Father, who art in Heaven
Hallowed be Thy Name
Thy Kingdom Come, Thy Will Be Done—

Seward exits. She continues for a moment.

On Earth, as it is in—

She watches the door as she gets up.

Heaven, give us this Day—

She inspects Lucy's body—and takes a ring, spots the necklace.

Our Daily—

She takes the necklace, inspects it, holds it up to the light.

(apologetically, to Lucy) Sorry, Miss. I really don't get paid enough.

She exits, pocketing the jewelry. A cold white light on Lucy, looking angelic. Somewhere church bells bong bong bong—the day is winding down. On Lucy's face, appears the smallest hint of a smile.

2.

RENFIELD:
    It has been almost a month—
    Since that terrible storm hit our shores.
    And the nights are growing
    —darker and thicker—
    Times are getting stranger and sicker
    In this sleepy seaside town.
    There is a kind of primordial—
    Disease come to newoldnewBritannia
    —a plague as in ancient times.
    People are dying in the night.
    They go to sleep
    Strong and hearty and hale—
    And in the morning are found
    Still and cooling and pale.
    A fisherman, a sensible fellow—
    Not given to wandering in the night—
    Is found down by the docks,
    Slumped against a wall, stark naked—
    Stiff—and damp—with dew.
    A housewife, a respectable matron,
    is left, stretched luxuriously—
    Face-down outside her front door—
    Her hand reaches back for the latch.
    Too late!
    And most shocking of all—
    Just last night—
    A little baby was stolen from her cradle.
    The mother is wild with grief and fear
    But there is no trace of the child.
    People are scared, people

Lock their doors and shut their windows tight,
but it is said that in the
Households visited by
This—misfortune—
The doors are unlocked, the windows are unbarred
From the *inside.*
The victims did it to themselves.
(*cheerfully*) I did warn you all!
I am sorry that you
Had no faith—and
You are paying the price.
Only through sacred suffering
May you learn to obey...!
Our Father, who art in Earth—

3.

Mina is with Jonathan—he is sitting up, looking better. She clears away a bowl.

JONATHAN:
Are you all right, Mina? You look—pale.

MINA:
—Me?
Things are—strange, and I have not been able to sleep since—Lucy. *(she stops herself)*
I'm not—supposed to speak of anything upsetting, until you are recovered.

JONATHAN:
—I am sure that will be soon.
And then—I will be—better than ever. I feel it, even now!

Beat.

MINA:
Jonathan—you haven't asked—about the baby, at all.

JONATHAN:
Oh. Yes. How—is it?

MINA:
Um.—Fine. *(lamely)* Do you want to—feel?

JONATHAN:
Fine. *(he touches her stomach. A weird, lame beat)* Mhm. Fine.

He removes his hand. She looks at him.

What?

MINA:
—you do not seem like yourself.

JONATHAN:
I have been ill.

MINA:
You don't remember—anything, about how you fell ill?

JONATHAN:
I remember—taking leave of you, and traveling through the Continent, until—the porters—*(he loses it)*. Old—stories—superstitions—*(he shakes his head to clear it)* whatever it is, I was lucky to escape. I don't want to think about it, any longer.

MINA:
Of course. *(she kisses him, begins to leave)*
Only—we don't even know if you concluded your business. Shouldn't you check on that?

JONATHAN:
My business?

MINA:
With that Count.

JONATHAN:
The Count—was a charming host.

MINA:
Yes, so you wrote—

JONATHAN:
I wrote you a—letter—but—
To—steal—and read a man's correspondence—

MINA:
What?

JONATHAN:
He—was handsome, and gracious. He—fed me well, he—

MINA:
Darling—

JONATHAN:
DON'T TOUCH ME!

MINA:
What?

JONATHAN:
DON'T YOU EVER BLOODY LISTEN?!! I SAID, YOU GET THE HELL AWAY FROM ME!

Van Helsing has entered. She has heard the end of it.

VAN HELSING:
—Mrs. Harker?—are you all right?

MINA:
—Doctor Van Helsing, this is my husband.

VAN HELSING:
That does not mean you are all right.

MINA:
—Jonathan, why don't you sit for a moment.

Jonathan sits, heavily.

He is recovering from a brain fever—I should not have provoked him.

VAN HELSING:
Uh-huh. *(she looks at her)*

MINA:
Doctor—you shouldn't be here, Seward has been organizing Lucy's affairs, we are guests in this house, and I do not wish to travel back to London yet, with Jonathan—so. So.

Jonathan flops flatly down on the bed, unnaturally, with a <u>grunt.</u> The women stand aside.

MINA:
Why are you here?

VAN HELSING:
Mrs. Harker—Mina. I need help in the watch, and I think you may have an aptitude for my line of work.

MINA:
Medicine?

VAN HELSING:
No. I want you to join the hunt for—the creatures who killed Lucy.

MINA:
Me.

VAN HELSING:
Why not you?

MINA:
I—I am in a family way.

VAN HELSING:
That doesn't stop your brain, does it? God knows, it shouldn't stop your life.

MINA:
But I do not want to—fight!

VAN HELSING:
The fight is here. Whether or not you want it—

MINA:
And—most of all, Van Helsing, I'm—terrified, terrified of those beings!

VAN HELSING:
Me, too.

She subconsciously traces her scar—then shakes it off.

There are monsters in this world, Mina.
Somebody has to stand against them.
Why not us?
Keep watch with me tonight.

MINA:
Watch what?

VAN HELSING:
You'll see.

Mina hesitates—then rouses Jonathan.

MINA:
Jonathan—I have to go out.

JONATHAN:
Mina—You were right.
I should check—upon my business.

He closes his eyes and seemingly falls asleep; Mina gathers her shawl to leave.

MINA:
At least let me know where we are headed, Doctor.

VAN HELSING:
You'll (see—)

MINA:
Van Helsing, if you give one more cryptic I-know-everything-and-you-know-nothing aren't-I-mysterious-and-impressive response I'm not going anywhere, and what's more I will sit down on this floor and scream and scream and SCREAM until I bloody well pass out.

VAN HELSING:
—Mina Harker. How *unladylike*.

MINA:
Oh, I'm (sorry)—

VAN HELSING:
I *love* it.

She starts to head out.

We are headed—*(she hoists a stake over her shoulder)* to Lucy's tomb.

4.

Outside Lucy's crypt, in the graveyard. Van Helsing is hanging a string of garlic.

MINA:
More garlic?

VAN HELSING:
I hang it here every day. But in the night, it's gone.

MINA:
Who is taking it down?

VAN HELSING:
Who, or what?

Van Helsing retreats from the crypt and sits on her haunches.

Here. *(she hands her a stake)*

MINA:
What am I supposed to (do with)—?

VAN HELSING:
Anything comes at you, stick it with the pointy end.

MINA:
Uh—

VAN HELSING:
Stop—listen. Something's coming.
Pointy end, Mina. Pointy end!
HOLD, DEM(ON)—

SEWARD:
AAHHH!

Seward is carrying a bouquet of flowers.

VAN HELSING:
SEWARD!

SEWARD:
You!

VAN HELSING:
What are you doing here?

SEWARD:
I am here to pay my respects!
What are YOU doing here?

MINA:
She is—visiting—Lucy's tomb.

SEWARD:
(to Van Helsing) Why can't you leave her—us—alone?
Don't think I don't know—who's been hanging this trash around here!

VAN HELSING:
And you have been taking it down.

SEWARD:
Mrs. Harker—I can't believe you would continue to assist this woman, after my express orders.

VAN HELSING:
My precautions are come to nothing. Those deaths are on my head.

MINA:
"Orders."

SEWARD:
I will have to dismiss you from my house, sick husband or no!

VAN HELSING:
(to Seward)—well, my head, and yours. You stubborn fool.

MINA:
(to Seward) Lucy's house. *(to Van Helsing)* Wait, what do you mean—deaths?

SEWARD:
All of her assets are mine, now.

MINA:
Lucky you!

SEWARD:
(to Van Helsing) And who are you calling a fool?

MINA:
You! You're the fool! That should be perfectly obvious by now!

SEWARD: I'm not the one who is following a maniac into graveyards, doing God knows what for God knows why—	**VAN HELSING:** Please /
SEWARD: I ought to have you both committed—	**VAN HELSING:** Please /

MINA:
I'd like to see you try!!!

VAN HELSING:
PLEASE! While you stand here squabbling, the danger is mounting!

SEWARD:
What *danger?*

VAN HELSING:
Seward—if you will not believe, except what you see with your own eyes—
—Come.

SEWARD:
Come where?

VAN HELSING:
Into the crypt.

SEWARD:
What?!!!

VAN HELSING:
If you want to know what happened to Lucy—you will find valuable—empirical—evidence within!

He still won't come.

You've seen—in the papers, that people are dying. We must stop infection from spreading.

He still won't come.

—If I'm wrong, Seward, you may lock me away in your asylum, and I will make no objection! I will sit quietly and breathe easily, and take a much-needed padded-cell holiday!

SEWARD:
Sounds like a plan.

VAN HELSING:
Mina. Let's go.

MINA:
Me?

VAN HELSING:
Who else?

MINA:
I don't think—

VAN HELSING:
—Yes, actually—you do.
Now come.

They begin to go; she hoists her lamp.

They enter the crypt, Van Helsing waving the lamp in front of them.

VAN HELSING:
Keep close.

It is very dark.

MINA:
(Mina gives a little scream and falls) Oh!

They all <u>freak out</u>—Van Helsing pulls out a stake and swings around the lamp wildly; Seward also swings his lantern around.

VAN HELSING:
What is it? Where is he?!!!!!

MINA:
No—no—it's not that!

SEWARD:
God, you scared me!

VAN HELSING:
Don't cry out unless you *mean* it!

MINA:
I'm sorry—I just—stumbled upon—?

She holds up a little tiny—something. It's so small.

SEWARD:
What is that?

MINA:
It's a shoe. A—little baby's shoe.

VAN HELSING:
Don't come any closer, no matter what happens.

She lights a sconce on the wall—or hangs the lantern on the wall—and Lucy is suddenly illuminated.

SEWARD:
—Lucy.

Lucy is still wrapped in those white, shrouded sheets, but they are stained with blood. And she looks—so beautiful—is bathed in white light. She seems to glow. Both Mina and Seward are inexpressibly moved—they loved her.

MINA:
She looks—

SEWARD:
—like—an angel.

VAN HELSING:
Not an angel.

MINA:
She looks—alive!

VAN HELSING:
Not alive.

SEWARD:
It's a miracle.

VAN HELSING:
Nope. *(she fingers her stakes, and pulls out a big silver crucifix)*

Seward has stepped forward.

—DO NOT get any closer.

The church bells ring—it is midnight.

Open your eyes, creature. I know you do not sleep.

Lucy sits up, smiling, and sucks blood off of her fingers.

LUCY:
Doctor Van Helsing. How lovely to see you again.

SEWARD:
Lucy!

VAN HELSING:
STAY BACK! *(she pushes George back; Mina pulls him back as well)*

LUCY:
George?—*(very convincing)* Oh, George, I am so frightened. There's been some—terrible mistake, I've been—trapped in here, buried alive!

SEWARD:
Lucy!

LUCY:
I am hungry, I am thirsty—won't you help me?

VAN HELSING:
(Van Helsing waves the crucifix at her) BACK!

SEWARD:
Lucy!

VAN HELSING:
This is not Lucy!

She touches Lucy with the crucifix; Lucy withdraws, hissing.

MINA:
Seward!!! Look!!!!

Lucy is backed onto the bier; she can't escape Van Helsing's crucifix; her face is animal, her movement, supernatural.

LUCY:
(panting, but turning her head at an unnatural angle to leer at Seward) Don't you—want my kisses, you big strong maaaan? *(she laughs)*

MINA:
Not Lucy!

LUCY:
(her eyes, fluttering, as if entering a trance) Come, husband—
Come, husband—
Come—COME

SEWARD:
She's calling me!

VAN HELSING:
Not you.

> *She brings the crucifix very close to Lucy; she is caught; Lucy hisses.*

He will not risk himself to save you. He is your possessor, not your paramour. He is not coming.

LUCY:
(her eye lids flutter) Do you think that you can stop it?

VAN HELSING:
I have before.

LUCY:
—yes—I can smell it on you *(she suddenly screams, terribly)* but, don't hurt me, a defenseless trembling girl! A harmless little woman!

VAN HELSING:
Not a woman.

LUCY:
(Van Helsing takes out her stake; Lucy screams again)
Have mercy!

VAN HELSING:
As you and yours had mercy on the people of Whitby? On an infant, stolen from its mother?

LUCY:
I only wanted to hold the baby—the sweet little baby—the tender juicy crunchy munchy baby—

SEWARD:
Oh, *God.*

LUCY:
Shh, George, shh! *(she twists her head and snarls at him)* Come and kiss me.

MINA:
Seward! Seward! Seward!

LUCY:
Give it up, now,—
Give in—

GIVE IT—

> *Against his will, Seward drifts towards her*

VAN HELSING:
(she pushes the crucifix down on Lucy; Lucy is burned and hisses, screaming)
Mina, hold him back!

LUCY:
Save me, George, save me from this—freak!
Help me—help me—help me!

VAN HELSING:
Mina, Seward—I would look away—

> *Van Helsing lays the crucifix on Lucy; it burns her, and she cannot move; it is like a weight on her chest. She is pinned down, panting.*

LUCY:
When my husband arrives—he will suck the marrow from your bones and lick the fat from your flesh and pluck the eyeballs from your skulls!

> *Van Helsing pulls out a large Bowie knife and tests the end of her stake, sharpening it.*

VAN HELSING:
—evocative.

LUCY:
Our Father
Who Art in Earth—

> *And with a huge overhand thrust, she plunges her stake into Lucy's heart; Lucy screams and thrashes, a horrible roaring keening animal scream, and vomits blood, and is gone. Van Helsing wipes a spatter of blood from her own face.*

VAN HELSING:
Now do you believe, Seward? Now—will you listen?

> *Seward throws up, noisily, and runs outside.*

Go after him.

> *Van Helsing picks up the big Bowie knife.*

MINA:
—What are you doing?!!

VAN HELSING:
—finishing the job.
You really won't want to see this part, Mina.

> *Mina leaves, horrified. Van Helsing looks down at Lucy.*
>
> *She lifts up the big Bowie knife, and takes a big fistful of Lucy's hair.*

5.

Lucy's house in Whitby. Van Helsing speaks as the scene transitions behind her:

VAN HELSING:
There are stories, you know—from every culture, every century. In Mesopotamia they've found shards of pottery, depicting demons drinking the blood of men. Babylonia had *Lilitu*, the wraith who ate infants. In China, *Jiangshi* stole life force; the Cherokee have a legend about *Jumlin*, the monster who craved flesh;— and just a decade ago in New England, there was a rash of people digging up grandma's corpse to make sure it stayed buried.
On and on and on—dismissed as the products of overactive imaginations or mass hysteria—there the creatures are:
Das wampir. Vampires.

SEWARD:
—vampires. They're just—

VAN HELSING:
Fairy tales? Ghost stories. Old wives' superstition. Modern men dismiss anything they
haven't discovered themselves!

SEWARD:
All right—

VAN HELSING:
/For most of history, the majority of people couldn't read or write! Doubly true for women. How could they pass down wisdom but by spoken word? It may get distorted over time, but if you listen to commonalities in the stories—you hear your
foremothers, whispering to you across the years.
So, *yes*, Seward, goddamned vampires.

MINA:
Are they,—demons?

VAN HELSING:
That's one theory. Some of my benighted *male* colleagues—

SEWARD:
/All *right*—

VAN HELSING:
/—posit that these creatures are a natural evolution of man. In order for that theory to be true, you must accept that to become the most vicious consumer is to become the highest self. But *I* have a new theory—a SUPERIOR theory—

SEWARD:
ALL *RIGHT*. God, I hate a lecture—

VAN HELSING:
That vampires are a parasitic species, which has always existed alongside humanity—feeding off of us, mimicking our behaviors, stealing our bodies—hiding in plain sight.

> *She absentmindedly feels her scar—as if it is paining her, or itching.*

The dangerous misconception,—is that they're fanged or pale or deformed. That you could identify one at a glance. But the monsters—look just like us.

MINA:
How did you become such an expert in this subject?

VAN HELSING:
(looking at Seward and Mina)—I have met one before.

> *Beat; her hand may stray, unthinkingly, to her scar—*

But that—my—vamp was young. Newly-made.

> *She shakes it off, clears her throat.*

Lucy's vamp spoke of an "old country." That means he's moved from place to place—
and they nest for centuries.
A vampire of that age is incredibly strong—he can bend minds; shape dreams; control those in weakened states. He is, truly, a monster in his prime—
And I mean to stop him.

SEWARD:
How do we do that?

VAN HELSING:
"We?"

SEWARD:
At this point, Van Helsing—you can say this—phenomenon is caused by—poltergeists, or hobgoblins, or tiny glowing worms from Planet Bellybutton.
Just tell me how to fight it.

VAN HELSING:
—you can follow my lead?

SEWARD:
I should have—heard you, earlier—maybe if I had, Lucy wouldn't be—.

Beat.

But she is, and if you're telling me that this—Thing is responsible, then I would like to help you kill that Thing.
Please and thank you.

Van Helsing nods—and hands him a stake—then turns to Mina and offers her a stake.

MINA:
Does it always have to end—like Lucy?

VAN HELSING:
It is destroy—or be destroyed.

SEWARD:
In Mrs. Harker's condition, Van Helsing—

VAN HELSING:
Do you think her condition melts her brain, Seward?
If she doesn't face this—her child will. *(she still holds out the stake to Mina)*

MINA:
(squaring her shoulders) How do we—destroy—them?

SEWARD:
The searing rays of the sun!

VAN HELSING:
Nope.
Why would a species dependent on passing as human, evolve to be allergic to daylight?

SEWARD:
The touch of a blessed crucifix!

VAN HELSING:
Wrong.
Christianity is dominant throughout much of the world. If religious paraphernalia did the job, vamps couldn't walk a city block without turning into ash.

MINA:
But you held down Lucy with a cross!

VAN HELSING:
A silver cross. SILVER is widely described in folklore as toxic to supernatural beings.

SEWARD:
Ah, yes, the purifying power of silver! I was going to say that next.

VAN HELSING:
It's not the symbols, it's the substance. That powder I threw in the face of his wives is silver dust, bought at considerable expense.
But silver—and garlic—are tools of deterrence, not destruction.
To keep them down—nothing beats a stake to the heart. (*she makes a demonstrative motion*) Decapitation seals the deal.

MINA:
Uch. (*she drops the stake*)

VAN HELSING:
(*she picks up the stake*) These are parasites—looking to establish a new colony of hosts.
We have to find the nest... before it's too late.

MINA:
How do we do that?

VAN HELSING:
I was hoping you might be able to tell me.

MINA:
Me?

VAN HELSING:

The vampire addressed you by name. He seemed to know you.

MINA:

—He—or something like him—was in my dreams. But it's all—cloudy.

VAN HELSING:

Vamps can mess up your memories, confuse your sense of reality. He must have compelled you to forget.

MINA:

I suppose so? I'm sorry—

VAN HELSING:

We'll have to find it another way. Seward, let's make a list / of local—

MINA:

—I just thought, at the time, that it was—nonsense—sparked by visiting that madwoman.

VAN HELSING:

Madwoman! *What.* Madwoman!!!!!!

6.

Van Helsing hurtles into Seward's asylum, followed by Seward and Mina; Miller is struggling with the keys.

VAN HELSING:
Why didn't you tell me about this before?!!

MINA:
I didn't think it was pertinent!

VAN HELSING:
Everything is pertinent, Mina!

SEWARD:
Van Helsing, you won't upset my patient too much, will you?

VAN HELSING:
Just the right amount.

SEWARD:
(to Mina) Renfield has been making progress, lately; she's stopped eating spiders!

MILLER:
Um, Doctor Seward—Renfield vomited up a great quantity of gory little feathers the other day.

SEWARD:
Feathers?

MILLER:
Believe she used the spiders to catch some sparrows, sir.

MINA:
Blugh.

MILLER:
But she hasn't done it since! Matter of fact, she hasn't done anything in the last week but stare at the wall and cry.

> *Renfield is indeed curled up, not facing them, perhaps in a bed— staring at the wall.*

SEWARD:
Renfield, you have visitors!

MINA:
Do you really think the ravings of this poor woman could help us find the vampire, Van Helsing?

SEWARD:
Renfield, won't you come out and say hello?

> *Renfield morosely rolls over and stares at Van Helsing, unblinking, for a moment. She is depressed.*

RENFIELD:
Hello, hunter.

VAN HELSING:
—I'd call that a big yes.

RENFIELD:
—Killer.
Murdered my Father's new wife, did you?
He is gonna be sooo maaaad.

VAN HELSING:
Renfield—we want to talk about the vampire.

> *Van Helsing is slowly approaching her, her hand reaching towards a pouch:*

RENFIELD:
"Vampire?"

VAN HELSING:
Blood-sucker. Life-eater.

RENFIELD:
Dirty words.

VAN HELSING:
Dirty work.

> *Van Helsing suddenly throws silver powder in her face.*

RENFIELD:
AHHHHhhhhHHHHHHHHHHH!
What did you do THAT for?

> *And then—Renfield spectacularly sneezes.*

VAN HELSING:
You're no vamp, then. Not even a vamp-in-training.

RENFIELD:
You got me all dusty!

VAN HELSING:
Just a brainwashed human thrall.
Pathetic.

RENFIELD:
"Pathetic?!!" I am his most beloved child!
And YOU have RUINED my SMOCK!

VAN HELSING:
Where is the nest, thrall?!!

RENFIELD:
You shall never find
What my Father wishes to remain hidden!

VAN HELSING:
People's lives are at sake!

RENFIELD:
If my Father teaches harsh lessons
It's only because he cares!

VAN HELSING:
Alright, enough talk—

> *She approaches Renfield, fist raised; Renfield freaks out, screaming merrily; a chase ensues, as this goes on—*

MINA:
You can't hurt her, she's sick!

SEWARD:
Stop, stop! You're making my asylum a madhouse!

VAN HELSING:
She's dangerous, she's complicit, she's his servant! So let me do what needs to be done! *(she approaches Renfield again)*

RENFIELD:
Help, help! Father! Strike them down! FATHER!

VAN HELSING:
Do you hear that??!!!

SEWARD:
Van Helsing /

VAN HELSING:
Destroy or be destroyed!!!

MINA:
Wait, Van Helsing, wait! Let me try!

> *She turns to Renfield, who briefly stops screaming—gesturing the other two back.*

—Hello, Renfield—remember me?

RENFIELD:
—Hello, little mother.
Do not let that hunter hurt me!!!!

MINA:
You're quite safe, I promise.

RENFIELD:
With her pointed sticks and terrible tricks!

> *She antagonizes Van Helsing, who heroically does not kill her.*

MINA:
Renfield—Renfield, please—I want to talk about—the vampire.

RENFIELD:
Nasty word! Vulgar term! <u>Potty talk!</u>

MINA:
Do forgive me—my—ignorance.
Can you educate me?

RENFIELD:
Really?

> *Mina nods.*

—you truly want to know?
Why?

MINA:
　—I—I could be ready—to—to join his—cause.

> *Renfield looks at her for a long moment—then suddenly LUNGES at her.*

RENFIELD:
　Oh. oh.
　Oh OH OH OH!

> *She springs and hugs her sloppily.*

SEWARD:
　RENFIELD, NO TOUCHING!

MINA:
　I'm all right!

> *Mina waves him off as Renfield babbles.*

RENFIELD:
　If I can bring him—
　A lovely creature like you—
　He must forgive me my trespasses!

MINA:
　What do you mean?

RENFIELD:
　I must have—sinned—terribly
　To be locked away here
　For so long!

MINA:
　What have you done wrong?

RENFIELD:
　He sent me ahead
　Before him.
　To Oldnewnewold Britannia
　To do His will.
　But Ladies cannot—you know—
　Sign deeds or buy property!
　I was turned away from every bank
　And court!
　I could not prepare His Kingdom!
　My vessel is too weak.
　So he has chosen another in my place!

I know He cannot help but act
With justice, but it is a harsh
Penance!

She cries.

MINA:

(Mina pats her back) Um—there, there *(Renfield blows her nose on Mina's sleeve)* —all right—

RENFIELD:

But perhaps if I can bring him a convert!!!!

MINA:

Tell me where I can find him, Renfield—
And I will give him what he is due.

RENFIELD:

Embrace religion,
Bow down and worship where you ought!
And he will find *you.*

Whispering Our Father Who Art in Earth.

SEWARD:

Now she's speaking in riddles.

MILLER:

When was she not speaking in riddles?

RENFIELD:

I practice so hard, little Mother—
I spread his Word,
I keep the faith, through many trials—
When will He make me in His Image?
What must I do to win his love?

MINA:

Is it so worth winning. You said your husband was—

RENFIELD:

A *baaaaad* man.

MINA:

—and you escaped that influence. Do you not want to do so again?

RENFIELD:

Can I tell you a secret?

Mina leans in—again, that harsh faux-whisper.

I escaped because my Father ATE my husband!

SEWARD:
Well, there's why we never found Mr. Renfield—

RENFIELD:
My husband was so much stronger than me but my Master was so much stronger than him—and it was HORRIBLE—all wet and red and crunching—

VAN HELSING:
Evocative—

RENFIELD:
—but then I thought, if it is consume or be consumed—and I fell down in worship, and He made me his disciple!
And if I do not give Him what He is due—I deserve to live bound, forever.

MINA:
This creature happened to save you, but that doesn't mean he is your savior. Maybe you don't have to obey anyone. Perhaps you can heal—and free yourself.

RENFIELD:
He has promised me
Salvation! Strength! Power!

MINA:
Those are just words. You may know him by his acts. A good man—

VAN HELSING:
Not—*man*

MINA:
—would not try your obedience at all! Why does he send you these trials? Is that the behavior of a loving Father?

RENFIELD:
He works—in mysterious ways!

MINA:
Why does he do terrible things to innocent creatures?

RENFIELD:
I am not fit—to question!

MINA:
Why not?
Test his hold over you. If he will not give you license within your own mind—what makes you think he will give you any liberty at all?

> *Renfield is stricken.*

VAN HELSING:
Where is he, Renfield?
Where is the nest?

RENFIELD:
(She looks at her, pants—once, twice, and then)—nnnnngghhh! NNnnnnNNNNNGGGGHHH!

> *Renfield holds her head, as if an icepick is drilling through her brain; she thrashes and screams, choking, under all of:*

MINA:
—what is happening to her?

VAN HELSING:
She is—actually testing his power. Well done, Mina—

SEWARD:
Is she all right?!!

VAN HELSING:
The bond between thralls and vamps is strong. Painful to strain. And if she can reach a bit
—into his mind, then I'm sure he can reach—

> *Renfield has suddenly sat up and is mouthing the words, like a dummy, but the voice is all:*

DRACULA:
Charming Mina Harker.

VAN HELSING:
BACK! EVERYONE BACK!

> *She shoves Mina away from Renfield.*

DRACULA:
The scarred hunter.
And Lucy Westenra's—impotent friend.

SEWARD:
Don't you speak her name!

DRACULA:
If you had any respect for the old ways, mortal—
You would be honored that I took her.
A virgin sacrifice.

Seward lunges at Renfield; Van Helsing holds him back.

VAN HELSING:
Seward!

DRACULA:
I licked up every drop
Before you could spoil her.

VAN HELSING:
Stop—he wants to make you hurt Renfield!

DRACULA:
She struggled just enough—
To give it flavor.

VAN HELSING:
She must hold some clue, to finding him!

DRACULA:
I can still taste her now—

SEWARD:
I'll kill you!

Van Helsing holds Seward back, as:

DRACULA:
Big promises from a weak modern man
She came to me—surrendered to me—
And I showed her who was *boyar*.

His voice begins to mount; Renfield moans under; Mina gets very close, staring into the eyes of the beast.

MINA:
We're going to run you into the ground, monster.

DRACULA:
Mina Harker—I will throw
Your child to my wives—I will suck

Renfield is screaming.

The marrow from your bones

> *Screaming.*

I will lick the fat from your skin

> *Screaming.*

I will pluck the eyeballs from your skull!

> *Screaming.*

VAN HELSING:
—enough.

> *She throws another puff of silver dust in Renfield's face. Dracula half-screams and disappears. Renfield collapses—*
> *—and then sneezes.*

RENFIELD:
*(recovering, to Van Helsing)—you—*are no fun at *all.*

MINA:
What was that word he said? *Boyar?*

SEWARD:
(to Van Helsing) Don't look at me, you're the language expert.

VAN HELSING:
Transylvanian: it means "lord." I'd say our vamp is Eastern European, despite the accent.

RENFIELD:
(re: the dust) Ooh, it's all sparkly.

MINA:
Transylvanian?

RENFIELD:
Look at my HAND!

VAN HELSING:
What?

MINA:
Nothing—only—if everything is pertinent—

RENFIELD:
Little mother—look at my hand!

MINA:
Come with me!!

> *They begin to exit; Renfield, frantically, after her—*

RENFIELD:
Little mother—wait—wait! *(she is waving her shining hand)*

MINA:
Yes—Renfield—that's very pretty.

RENFIELD:
No—
How can you truly tell—a good being from a bad?
How do you know if you are cherished or loved
—Or only tricked?

>*Mina has no answer for her.*

VAN HELSING:
(offstage) Mina!

>*Renfield is left looking through her bars—her shining hands on them, as if to gild them—*

7.

Mina takes Seward and Van Helsing to Jonathan's room; Jonathan is disturbed, manically getting dressed, humming to himself, packing things away.

VAN HELSING:
Transylvania? Your husband fell ill in Transylvania?!! NOBODY THINKS TO TELL ME THESE THINGS?

MINA:
—the doctor said he wasn't to be disturbed with questions about that time, or he would never heal!

SEWARD:
Don't fix me with that searing cowboy stare, Van Helsing, it wasn't my recommendation.

They enter the room. Jonathan is buzzing back and forth.

MINA:
Jonathan—*(surprised)* you're up and about.

JONATHAN:
Mina, we must go back to London.

MINA:
When?

JONATHAN:
Now. I have business to do, as you so helpfully reminded me. And I'm feeling much stronger.

MINA:
I can see that.

JONATHAN:

Mina *(he snaps at a waiting bag; Mina recoils at the snap)*
Pack. We have intruded on Doctor Seward's hospitality long enough. *(he finally sees Seward and Van Helsing)*

MINA:

You remember Doctor Van Helsing, Jonathan.
I need you to tell her—what you can remember of your time in Transylvania.

He stills.

JONATHAN:

Transylvania? I don't want to talk about that.

VAN HELSING:

Why were you there?

JONATHAN:

/—Mina, come on—

MINA:

He was meeting with a Count to arrange—the purchase of properties.

VAN HELSING:

What *Count*?

JONATHAN:

The Count—was a charming and gracious host. A handsome man—he fed—me well—

MINA:

/Jonathan—

JONATHAN:

/And my business with him is unfinished!
We must go to London!

MINA:

Jonathan—just calm down, and tell /us—

JONATHAN:

Mina! SHUT UP AND PACK! DON'T MAKE ME TELL YOU AGAIN!

A shocked silence. Seward steps forward.

JONATHAN:
Don't you dare step between me and my wife, Seward, I have a right to command her.

MINA:
Jonathan—you are not yourself.

> *Jonathan is advancing on them; Van Helsing slowly, casually, is taking off one of her ever-present silver necklaces.*

VAN HELSING:
Hold it right there, Harker—

JONATHAN:
MINA!

VAN HELSING:
Let me—try something.

> *Van Helsing very gently raises the silver necklace towards Jonathan.*

JONATHAN:
What is that?

VAN HELSING:
Just a trinket.

JONATHAN:
What—what are you doing?

VAN HELSING:
An experiment.

> *She very, very gently presses the necklace against Jonathan's forehead, and he SCREAMS—*

VAN HELSING:
Thought so.

> *He's still screaming, screaming; Van Helsing presses the silver against him.*

MINA:
You're hurting him!

VAN HELSING:
Not him.
Jonathan Harker, are you in there?

Jonathan screams.

JONATHAN:
(*Jonathan thrashes, his eyes rolling, as if having a religious fit*) He is—coming!!!—He is—come!!!

VAN HELSING:
I know, buddy.

Jonathan writhes up again.

Down!

She presses him down; he collapses—Mina runs to him.

MINA:
What did you do?!!!

VAN HELSING:
Returned him to you. For now.

Jonathan moans: his voice is very different now.

JONATHAN:
—what *was* that—

Jonathan turns toward her—his forehead is marked with a bright red, terrible burn.

MINA:
—Your forehead!

JONATHAN:
(*coming to*) M- Mina?!! Where am I?

MINA:
You're in—the guest bedroom, in—

JONATHAN:
In Britain? In Whitby? (*clutching at her, panicking*) Mina—he's here—he came to get Miss Westenra!

SEWARD:
Lucy?

JONATHAN:
He was controlling me—he made me do terrible things!

VAN HELSING:
Who did?

JONATHAN:
The Count.
Count Dracula.

VAN HELSING:
(this is a new name to her:) Dracula.

JONATHAN:
What has been happening? I can't—everything has been so cloudy. And my head hurts, something awful—

SEWARD:
Let me examine you, Harker.

> *Seward examines him, not very effectively. Van Helsing takes Mina aside.*

MINA:
What is wrong with him? Is he—like Renfield?

VAN HELSING:
Worse.
He's been bitten.

MINA:
Bitten?

VAN HELSING:
He's infected.
If we don't stop this Dracula—your husband will turn.

> *Seward sits Jonathan back up.*

JONATHAN:
Thank God you did that, Madame—

VAN HELSING:
Doctor—

JONATHAN:
Doctor—it's the only way I could break free.

MINA:
What do you mean?

JONATHAN:
I was myself, but not myself—it's like the shell of me was talking to you, and this other—force was operating me. Like—

VAN HELSING:

A parasite?

> *He nods.*

VAN HELSING:

(celebrates) Yes! YES YES YES! *(everybody is staring at her)* Sorry. A couple of extremely condescending, cocksure colleagues now owe me an exorbitant amount of money. *(she clears her throat)* Go on.

MINA:

—how did you even get here, from Transylvania? How did you escape the count?

JONATHAN:

I—I don't remember. He must have made me forget.

VAN HELSING:

Tell me about the "business" this Dracula wanted you to conduct.

JONATHAN:

I—don't—don't recall—

VAN HELSING:

Do you have any memory of where these properties he wanted to purchase were?

JONATHAN:

I—don't—know—I—I—

> *Jonathan's eyes start fluttering; he is having a fit.*

SEWARD:

Harker!

JONATHAN:

IiIiI'm gonna get in such trouble
Tatt-ling!
Daddy is—coming

> *Jonathan screams.*

MINA:

Jonathan!

VAN HELSING:

Not Jonathan.

> *Jonathan sits up—but again, just as it was with Renfield, it is all:*

Count Dracula, I presume.

DRACULA:
Another little eye, spying?
One more peasant, rising up against me?
A clever Killer—
Leading the revolution?
I wished to live quietly
I wished to disappear
But if it is war—
Than I shall conquer
I will take no prisoners alive,
You impudent, sniveling little—!

VAN HELSING:
We get it.

She presses the silver against Jonathan again; he screams.

Out! Out!

He screams and collapses.

MINA:
(to Jonathan) Are you all right?

JONATHAN:
(EXTREMELY over being possessed—and this is a ridiculous question) <u>NO!</u>
He just took over again, like I was—nothing.
I was able to fight him off, but—only because he's far enough
away—if he were here, I don't know if I could—resist.

VAN HELSING:
—what do you mean, he was far away?

SEWARD:
How could Harker know that?

VAN HELSING:
If Dracula could see through him, perhaps he could see through
Dracula. The parasite / host relationship is often reciprocal—like
in pregnancy, Mina; the child gives you certain things, even as it
leeches from you.

MINA:
Please do not call my baby a parasite.

VAN HELSING:
(to Jonathan) Did you get any impression of where the Count was
when he was—in you?

JONATHAN:
> It was dark—dusty—I smelled—death—old and new—and—a kind of—smoke. Stone—and candles—*and*—*(he is slipping under again)* Our Father, who art in Earth—

MINA:
> JONATHAN!
> GET *(slap)* IT *(slap)* TOGETHER! *(she slaps him, hard; he comes back to Earth)*

> *A shocked beat of silence.*

SEWARD:
> —Mrs. Harker!
> What a *backhand*.

JONATHAN:
> —sorry. Sorry—I'm here. *(he holds his head)* sorry.

VAN HELSING:
> —I know where the nest is!

SEWARD:
> Where?

VAN HELSING:
> Shush. *(she puts a finger to her lips, looking at Jonathan)*

SEWARD:
> "Shush"?

VAN HELSING:
> I'll tell you later. *(looking at Jonathan)* We don't know exactly who is listening.

JONATHAN:
> I beg your pardon.

VAN HELSING:
> Either you're too weak to resist him, Harker—

MINA:
> Van Helsing!

VAN HELSING:
> Or you're, in some way, complicit! We don't know how much of it is compulsion, and how much of it is choice!

JONATHAN:
—You don't know me, Doctor—but I am—I was a—good man.
Don't tell me where the nest is. I don't—want to know... anything.

> *Jonathan goes off and sits on the bed; Mina, royally irritated at Van Helsing, sits by him.*

VAN HELSING:
Let's hunt.

> *Seward nods, then—*

Mina—are you ready?

MINA:
Me?

VAN HELSING:
You.

> *She flips her a stake.*

Stick 'em with the pointy end.

> *Mina, having nowhere else to put it, sticks it awkwardly in her belt. As she does:*

MINA:
What about Jonathan?

VAN HELSING:
We need to keep him somewhere secure—somewhere he can be restrained, if necessary.
Seward—could we have him committed?

MINA:
No!

JONATHAN:
—you want to put me in an asylum?

SEWARD:
—he'd have attendants there, who can raise alarms.

VAN HELSING:
Even if he is mostly himself—

MINA:
Van Helsing, he is!

VAN HELSING:
—Dracula will almost certainly try to influence him again. He'll be safest if he's—contained.

JONATHAN:
Do it, Mina. Put me away.
I feel mad enough.

8.

> *The asylum. Miller lets them into a space next to Renfield's. Renfield lies unmoving, facing the wall.*

SEWARD:
—It's not so bad, is it?

JONATHAN:
It's not so good.

SEWARD:
Renfield! I have brought you a neighbor.

MILLER:
She hasn't moved since you left, Doctor.

MINA:
Renfield! It's Mina Harker.

> *Renfield doesn't move.*

Renfield.

> *No response; Van Helsing shrugs.*

JONATHAN:
Doctor—I insist that you do tie me up.

SEWARD:
This is not that kind of institution.

JONATHAN:
If Dracula reaches me—I might do harm.

> *Seward hesitates.*

Please.

SEWARD:
　Miller—

　　　　Miller scuttles off.

MINA:
　Jonathan—I have to go fight.

JONATHAN:
　What? Mina, it's not safe—

MINA:
　No place is safe.
　And our child will face monsters if I don't.
　Are you still going to try and keep me back?

JONATHAN:
　—Not anymore.

　　　　She kisses him, as Miller ties his hands. They exit.

　　　　Miller clangs the door shut. A moment, two—it is dark and fairly horrible in the asylum. Jonathan sits, his hands bound.

JONATHAN:
　Our Father, who art in Heaven—

　　　　He drops his head.

RENFIELD:
　That's not how it goes!

　　　　She rolls over, smiling.

　Hello, Brother.

JONATHAN:
　No—no—no

RENFIELD:	**JONATHAN:**
Our Father, who art in Earth—	Help—help!
Of Earth, and by Earth—	

　　　　He clangs against the bars, frantically—

RENFIELD:	**JONATHAN:**
Lousy tattletale,	HELP!
Disobedient brat!	

The mist, that strange mist is gathering all around them—as it did when Lucy disappeared.

RENFIELD:
Daddy, I welcome you in!
I, your Renfield,
I accept your Spirit into this place!

Miller has run back in—angrily:

MILLER:
Oy, oy, what's all this, then?

JONATHAN:
Oh God, Oh God, no—

RENFIELD:
(Ecstatically) He is coming—

JONATHAN:
He is coming—

RENFIELD AND JONATHAN:
He is come!

A beat of pure silence—Jonathan is frozen, like a rabbit under a hawk.

MILLER:
What's all this noise, maniacs? Hm? Renfield?

She pauses in front of her—she is facing out, her face shining.

For once, you have nothing to say?

RENFIELD:
(in a state of breathless religious ecstasy) I am struck dumb in His Presence!
Naughty child—
Bow down and worship, and you still may yet be saved!

MILLER:
What does that mean, nutjob? Eh? Speak up.

And right behind Miller, right behind her, materializing as if out of nowhere—is Dracula.

RENFIELD:
Sorry, Miller.
I did warn you.

Miller turns—and faces Dracula. Miller begins to scream—and Dracula casually, swiftly tears out Miller's throat. Miller chokes on her own blood, and drops.

RENFIELD:
Father! I knew that you would come!

Dracula smilingly steps over Miller's body and walks into Jonathan's cell.

JONATHAN:
No—no—

DRACULA:
Poor Jonathan Harker. Trussed up like a holiday ham. *(he smells)* Delicious.

JONATHAN:
No—

DRACULA:
No?

He lays hands on Jonathan, breaking his barriers—Jonathan tries to resist—

JONATHAN:
N—n—

DRACULA:
Shhhhhhh—
No more refusing me, sweetheart.
Not ever again.
Now—what did you say?

JONATHAN:
Y-Yes.

DRACULA:
Yes.

He casually begins to take off Jonathan's ropes; as he does:

RENFIELD:
Father!
Will you not lay your hands upon *me*?

DRACULA:
Shh, Renfield. Be quiet.

RENFIELD:
Yes, Father. I will stop talking, Father. Only I am so excited, Father!
Where are we going? Only tell me where we are going,
And I will be quiet as a little mouse.

DRACULA:
Shhh—

RENFIELD:
Shhhh—(*she tries to imitate him, but is too excited*)
I knew you would loose our bonds, Master!

DRACULA:
Come, Jonathan.

> *He walks out; Jonathan rises and follows—right past Renfield's cell. Dracula does not stop.*

RENFIELD:
Father? (*Dracula is still walking out*)
PLEASE!
Please don't test me any more!
I am sorry, I am sorry—set me free!

DRACULA:
Free?

RENFIELD:
Bring me home! Break me out from this place!
Give me strength and power
So mortal men may never hold me again!

> *He comes to her bars.*

DRACULA:
You wish to become like me, Renfield?

RENFIELD:
Oh, yes—please—make me in your Image
I have worked so hard to prove I am worthy—
I have listened in the dark, I have preached your Word—

DRACULA:
You have not been useful!
Not as you should have been!

RENFIELD:
I can do better—
—I can be—whatever you wish me to be—

> *He makes no movement to free her; she is frightened.*

Will you not have faith,
As I have had faith in you?
Father—I am—your most favored child—

DRACULA:
Shhh.
Listen carefully now, Renfield.
You are not my child.
I am not your Father.
You were my servant.
And you fell short.
You were tested.
And you *failed*.
You could not finish my business.
You could not spread my word in this new land
Your vessel is too weak.
So eat all the crawling creatures you want—
You will creep no higher than they do.

RENFIELD:
Father—

DRACULA:
Renfield—you were never good enough.

RENFIELD:
Master—Father—Daddy!
HAVE MERCY, PLEASE!

> *Dracula, very casually, throws the rope from Jonathan's hands down, just by her cell bars.*

DRACULA:
Free yourself.

> *He walks out; Jonathan follows. Neither of them look back. Renfield is left completely alone, completely broken. Miller's dead body. The asylum is so quiet, now. Renfield sits, then reaches out as if to touch Miller—to pet her hair.*

RENFIELD:

.....

....

....

Miller?
Miller, I am sorry.
But I mean it this time.
I am sorry, little mother.
I fell for the pretty words.
Thought if I only gave—I should receive.
Silly sentimental Renfield.
I should have opened my eyes.

> *She reaches again for Miller—but this time, her hand closes on the rope. She grabs it, and brings it in to her, as she speaks. She walks to her bed.*

Do you know—I cannot even remember what my name was before Mrs. Renfield, Miller?
Who I was
Before I forgot my self
Before I sacrificed my name, my body, my soul, to gain the approval of masters of earth—
But—

> *She takes the rope and hangs it from a rafter. She begins to make a noose. As she does:*

Why should I have a name.
Flies do not have names,
Nor spiders,
Nor sparrows!
I would have their lives,
And forget my trespasses
I would belong to no one—
And follow no rules—
Open the windows—
Break down the bars—

> *She slips the noose around her neck.*

I would be free!

> *She steps forward. The lights go out.*

9.

The churchyard; those same old graves. Van Helsing lays out a pile of stakes.

VAN HELSING:
I'll ration out the silver powder.

Van Helsing goes to pour out the powder in little sacks; Seward goes to hand Mina stakes.

SEWARD:
Mrs. Harker.

MINA:
Sorry. My mind is—elsewhere.

She takes the stakes.

SEWARD:
—your husband?

MINA:
You have to understand, Doctor Seward—Jonathan is—was—gentle and kind and stable—I once thought I could foretell every movement he ever made.
But—all men may be unknowable, in the end.

SEWARD:
Mrs. Harker—

MINA:
We may be about to die, Seward. You can call me Mina.

SEWARD:
—if you call me George.
I'm sure your Jonathan was—is—a decent fellow. Once Dracula's influence over him is broken, he'll go back to what he was.

MINA:
You are given so much power over us. It is difficult not to live in fear.

SEWARD:
Still.
I wish, you know—that Lucy—had trusted me—with her self. With who she truly was. Even those fears. I did not need her to meet—whatever expectations she thought I had.
We are not all monsters.

MINA:
The problem, sir, is that it's hard to tell which ones will consume you.

SEWARD:
There are good men in this world, Mina Harker.
I shall prove it to you.

> *He hoists the stakes, and salutes Van Helsing, who approaches with the little sacks of powder.*

VAN HELSING:
(Van Helsing distributes the powder) Aim for the eyes.

SEWARD:
Van Helsing—where in the—*(looking at Mina)* h-e-l-l are we going?

VAN HELSING:
Even I, Seward—even I am swayed by the old symbols and superstitions. Even I am capable of thinking that no evil can flourish under those signs, though evidence is decidedly to the contrary—

SEWARD:
Wonderful, more speaking in riddles—

VAN HELSING:
Some part of me did not think they would desecrate—but of course, it's obvious—

MINA:
WHERE, Van Helsing?

VAN HELSING:
Dracula lies, Mina Harker—with the bride of Christ.

MINA:
The nest—is in the church?

SEWARD:
The CHURCH? Jesus.

VAN HELSING:
—Sure.
Lucy, Renfield, your husband all raved about our Father, conversion, salvation. Renfield told you to "embrace religion." It was before us, the whole time.
The vamps are hiding in the crypts, if I had to guess. Dark, rarely visited. Comfortable enough, if one is accustomed to dusty Romanian castles.

SEWARD:
Well, then.

He hoists another stake.

Let us pray.

10.

A great cacophony of church bells. Lanterns aloft, they begin to enter the crypt.

VAN HELSING:
Stakes out.
(to Seward) There should be another entryway from the back, under the altar.
Work your way towards us.

SEWARD:
We'll meet in the middle.

VAN HELSING:
(she holds out her hand to shake) Godspeed—Doctor Seward.

SEWARD:
Thank you—*Doctor* Van Helsing.

They shake. He kisses Mina's hand, smiling—and exits.

VAN HELSING:
Stay close.

Mina and Van Helsing advance into the crypt, their lanterns aloft; it is dark and dusty and full of shadows; the perfect place for an ambush. After a few moments, Mina suddenly squeaks—her voice so full of terror, she can hardly get sound out.

MINA:
Errrrrk!

Van Helsing swings her lantern around quickly—and the light shines on Marilla and Drusilla, curled in a pile across the room. They are stained with blood, their eyes closed, lightly, non-sexually draped on each other—totally still. They look like nothing so much as a pair of kittens, napping. A beat. Two. Marilla and Drusilla are like statues.

VAN HELSING:
(*as they move forward*) Shh—

DRUSILLA:
(*eyes still closed*) Shhh—

MARILLA:
(*eyes still closed*) / Shhh—

VAN HELSING:
Shhhhiit.

> *Drusilla stirs a little—again, rather like a kitten dreaming—and settles.*
>
> *Marilla and Drusilla sit up.*

DRUSILLA:
(*they languidly stretch and yawn, opening their eyes*) Mmmmm, I can smell it, Marilla—

MARILLA:
(*it's going to be a beautiful day*) Me too, Drusilla—

DRUSILLA:
(*they might as well be at a spa*) Breakfast in bed.

> *She turns and smilingly looks upon Van Helsing and Mina.*
>
> *Marilla turns and looks at them.*

MARILLA:
Hello, little mother—

DRUSILLA:
Scarred-up hunter—

MARILLA:
You're certainly asking for it.

> *Drusilla and Marilla slowly, slowly work their way across the room—it is all languid and unhurried.*

DRUSILLA:
It's your own fault, darlings—

MARILLA:
Coming in here—

DRUSILLA:
Dressed like that—

MARILLA:
Looking so good

DRUSILLA:
Don't you want our kisses? Don't you want us to make you feel

MARILLA:
Big and strong—
Put that nasty stick down—

> *Van Helsing's stick seems to falter; is she being hypnotized? Drusilla is going to Van Helsing—Marilla, to Mina.*

DRUSILLA:
You know you want it:

DRUSILLA AND MARILLA:
Give in, now,—
Give in to us—
GIVE IT—

VAN HELSING:
Ladies—
We are not your target audience.

> *Van Helsing strikes; Mina throws silver powder in Drusilla's face. Marilla and Drusilla shriek—Van Helsing goes down, struggling with Marilla—she's just missed; Mina is standing over Drusilla, who has been blinded by the powder.*

VAN HELSING:
Strike, Mina! Mina, strike!

> *Marilla attacks her; they struggle, rolling around on the floor.*

DRUSILLA:
Please—don't, I can be saved!
I don't want to be a monster!

> *Van Helsing gives Marilla a death blow, but is herself knocked out; both Marilla and Van Helsing lie still; Drusilla gets to her knees.*

MINA:
Stay right there! *(she holds the stake over her)*
Van Helsing!
VAN HELSING!

> *No response.*

> *She raises the stake to strike.*

DRUSILLA:
I am just a woman like you—I was scared, I was hungry, and he deceived me—I am a victim, don't hurt me, help me—help me—

> *Mina starts to lower the stake—and Drusilla grabs it, and throws it away. Now Mina is completely defenseless. She backs away from her. Drusilla advances.*

Stupid little girl.
Heeding easy words.
We could have given you death sweetly,
We could have made it good.
But now—
Now, you're going to p—

> *Van Helsing has popped up behind Drusilla—and stabs her through the heart, through the back, she shrieks and dies, collapsing.*

VAN HELSING:
MINA. NOT A WOMAN.

MINA:
(shaking) Oh God.

VAN HELSING:
These creatures are adaptive parasites, conditioned to do his will! They have no relationship with the truth, they'll say anything to make you confused—and then press the advantage.
Next time I tell you strike, do not hesitate!

MINA:
(still shaking) I don't think—I can—kill like that, Van Helsing—I am—not a fighter—

VAN HELSING:
Become one!

MINA:
—I can't.

> *Van Helsing looks at her, nods. Disappointed. She picks up Mina's stake, and puts it in her own belt.*

VAN HELSING:
—then at least take the watch.

> *They cast around—but all is silent, cold, and silent.*

MINA:
But—if this is the nest—where is Dracula?

SEWARD (O/S):
VAN HELSING!

They run out.

11.

> *They run into the church—Seward is circling the altar. And right in front of the altar—is Dracula. Seward does not dare take his eyes off of Dracula.*

SEWARD:
VAN HELSING!

VAN HELSING:
I'm here, Seward!

SEWARD:
This is—Count Dracula, I presume? If not—I am being wildly offensive to the rector.

> *Mina runs in, and quickly checks herself.*

DRACULA:
Dear Doctor Cuckold! Mina Harker! And the scarred-up hunter! What a delightful party.
If only sweet Lucy could join us—but you're to blame for that, Van Helsing.

SEWARD:
Don't you speak her name!

DRACULA:
(smacking his lips) Juicy Lucy.

VAN HELSING:
Slow, Seward. He's baiting you.

DRACULA:
You smell of blood, Van Helsing.

> *He sniffs; casually.*

You killed my wives, I suppose?
My poor little sweetlings?

SEWARD:
Don't get too close, Mina—

DRACULA:
A pity. But I will make more.

SEWARD:
—It's not just him up there!

DRACULA:
Mina Harker cannot replace her spouse so easily.

> *He raises a hand—and Jonathan steps forth. He stands, staring at them—docile as a cow.*

MINA:
Jonathan!

DRACULA:
Such a delightful party.

MINA:
Jonathan, get away from him! *(she screams) Jonathan!*

DRACULA:
Smile, Jonathan. You're so pretty when you smile.

> *Jonathan obediently smiles; the smile stays on his face; Dracula caresses him.*

MINA:
Let him go!

DRACULA:
Alas, I cannot. He has business to complete for me—in London.

VAN HELSING:
London?

DRACULA:
Do you think I would make my nest in this sleepy little seaside town, Hunter?
I am only—on holiday.
Jonathan Harker is in the process of securing me properties in Londinium—a worthy hunting ground.

SEWARD:
God.

DRACULA:
Almost!
I will live in the great city, one amongst many!
(as he says this, Jonathan's mouth also moves—he is overtaken) I will disappear, with my Englishmun as host. And we shall see how a *boyar* may rule, from the shadows. *(together with Jonathan)* What the masses may do.

SEWARD:
A parasite blending into a population that large—

VAN HELSING:
He'll infect—thousands. Tens of thousands.

DRACULA:
"*Parasite?*" I am your master, I am your Lord, you should bow down and worship me as your—

SEWARD:
—God I hate a lecture!

> *Seward runs forward and throws the silver dust on Dracula—*

DRACULA:
(as if he is burning; Seward gets closer, stake raised)
Ah—ahhhhHHH
—ahchoo.

> *Seward is right there, Moving—so fast—he grabs Seward by the throat.*

VAN HELSING:
SEWARD!

DRACULA:
I am old. Do you think diversions stop me? NOTHING can stop me!

> *Where his throat is pierced by Dracula's nails, Seward has begun to bleed—Dracula hisses and goes in to bite.*

Fee fi fo fum—

> *Van Helsing roars and runs in, stakes raised—Dracula throws Seward across the room and easily avoids Van Helsing. Seward hits a wall with incredible force and slumps.*

MINA:
SEWARD!

DRACULA:
Too slow.

> *Jonathan stares at her, that smile on his face. Mina runs to Seward and stands over him, with his fallen stake—Van Helsing and Dracula circle each other.*

DRACULA:
Where is the cavalry, Van Helsing?
What does one scarred-up woman hope to accomplish—with tricks and pointed sticks?

VAN HELSING:
We'll see.

> *Van Helsing swings—Dracula easily evades.*

DRACULA:
Try again.

> *Van Helsing swings—and misses.*

Again.

> *Van Helsing swings—and misses.*

Again.

> *Van Helsing swings—and misses—she is getting tired.*

Do you think this is my first encounter?

> *Van Helsing swings—and misses.*

I have fed on many a brave young killer.

> *Van Helsing swings—and misses.*

I will allow that you are my first lady hunter! And it—is—

> *Van Helsing stumbles.*

aDORable. Times, they *do* change!

> *Dracula quite casually swings her into a wall.*

VAN HELSING:
(*grunting*) I am no Lady—

DRACULA:

Oho. Do you think, that because *(imitating her accent)* you dress tough, and talk rough, that none of the rules apply to you? That you can stand against natural order?

VAN HELSING:

(swing and a miss)—I have stood before.

DRACULA:

Against a youngling, scarcely reborn. *(he hits her, hard)* Daddy's here.

VAN HELSING:

(so tired, so angry, with her last strength) You are not—Our Father. You are not superior. You are not—a being to be worshipped!

DRACULA:

What dangerous ideas, Hunter. For you. *(as he says this, he very easily beats Van Helsing, smacking her around, taking her stakes)*

VAN HELSING:

Mina!

> *He hits her hard; so hard she doubles over in terrible pain.*

DRACULA:

Don't cry on the job, honey, nobody will take you seriously.

> *He hits her hard, then takes her face in his hands.*

VAN HELSING:

MINA! DO SOMETHING!

> *Dracula hits Van Helsing hard, and she goes down—she is now on the ground.*

DRACULA:

(he turns towards Mina, who still stands over Seward)
Charming Mrs. Harker. You fragile harmless flower. You delicate little lady.
I'm going to rip the child from her womb, Hunter, and suck the pulp of it before your eyes.

MINA:

Get away!

DRACULA:

(still to Van Helsing) Because you must be shown, Van Helsing—that you cannot overturn thousands of years of tradition. You cannot tear down all of the old ways, alone.

> *He advances.*

Mina, Mina, Mina. Not my taste—but I'm going to make an exception.

JONATHAN:
N—no.

> *Jonathan is trying so hard, so hard to break free; he can't move, but he is shaking with it; Dracula turns around and moves towards Jonathan, on the altar.*

DRACULA:
What?

JONATHAN:
N—NO—

DRACULA:
"No?" We discussed that word.

JONATHAN:
Please—stop

> *Dracula is closer and closer to Jonathan.*

DRACULA:
All this rebellion, all these senseless new ideas, these would-be coups—I am really getting—annoyed—

JONATHAN:
S—stop.

> *Dracula takes Jonathan by the collar, dragging him, right up to his face.*

DRACULA:
Jonathan—sweetheart—you don't quite understand. Beings like myself have shaped mankind since your ancestors' ancestors crawled out of bogs! You cannot deny me; you cannot resist me; because YOU *ARE* ME. Even if you struck me down, I would rise! You would resurrect me YOURSELF—because I am the pinnacle of YOUR EVOLUTION! You may JOIN ME or you may BECOME MEAT, YOU MAY CONSUME or BE CONSUMED; but you cannot hope to OVERTHROW YOUR OWN NATURE! ***SOME THINGS—SHALL NEVER—CHANGE!***

> *He is about to bite—*

VAN HELSING:
  MINA! STRIKE!

DRACULA:
  Mi—/

> *He whirls around to where Mina last was—but unseen, Mina has crept up behind him and Jonathan; when he turns—she STRIKES. She stabs him, right through the heart. He screams, a big ancient animal unearthly scream. She stabs him again and again and again. On the altar. Before the cross. As she does, with each swing.*

MINA:
  NO!
  NO!
  NO!
  <u>WE! SAID! NO!!!!!</u>

> *She delivers the final death below. Dracula screeches—in his scream are all the screams ever caused, every life he has ever taken—and collapses on the altar. A big sound, as if all the air has been sucked out of the room, as if a portal opened to hell—and then it's gone. Mina stands, swaying; his dark blood is all over her, staining her.*

VAN HELSING:
  (sitting up, painfully)—I never said—I would do it—alone. *(she spits at Dracula's corpse)* ...Jackass.

> *Beat.*

MINA:
  God.

VAN HELSING:
  Evidently not.

> *Van Helsing drags herself up.*

MINA:
  I—I didn't hesitate.

VAN HELSING:
  I saw.

MINA:
  Jonathan! *(she runs to him)*

VAN HELSING:
  (re: Jonathan)—careful!

MINA:
Are you all right?

JONATHAN:
(he touches her face) —yes.
Doctor Van Helsing. I'm all right.

> *Van Helsing looks at him—and gives one tight nod. He leans in and kisses Mina—suddenly—they all start in horror.*

DRACULA:
(broken, from the ground—almost a wheeze)
You—impudent—brats—

> *He crawls slowly along the ground, like a great worm or a dying insect, trailing a great wash of dark blood, a nightmare creature.*

I will suck the marrow—from your bones—and lick the fat—from your flesh and pluck the eyeba/lls—

VAN HELSING:
Shush.

> *Astride him, she stabs down once more with a big stake; Dracula gurgles and dies.*
>
> *She whips out her big Bowie knife to decapitate him, when—a groan.*

MINA:
Seward!

> *They all rush to him.*

VAN HELSING:
Let me examine him.

> *She gently examines him; Seward gasps. A long beat—she sits back, grim-faced; a trickle of blood is coming from his mouth.*

VAN HELSING:
—I've seen worse, my friend.

> *It's very painful for him to talk.*

SEWARD:
"Friend?" Now—I know—I'm finished.

VAN HELSING:
You'll be up on your feet in no time!

SEWARD:
Van Helsing—you—are—truly—mad.

> *He closes his eyes. Mina kneels by his side. Van Helsing shakes her head no.*

SEWARD:
Mrs.—Harker.

MINA:
(through her tears) I told you to call me Mina.

SEWARD:
Mina—*(she takes his hand; he's smiling, painfully, it's a bit of a joke)* Did I prove to you—there is—a good—man?

MINA:
Yes—George.
You win.
We—we've won, George—? *(she's crying; his eyes are closed; she's trying to reach him—)* we've won—we've

VAN HELSING:
Mina.
It's too late.

> *She takes off her hat.*
>
> *Seward's body lies still; there is a great cacophony of church bells. The faithful are called to services. The lights fade.*

12.

The bells continue as we transition; a few weeks later. Van Helsing, her arm in a sling, bids goodbye to Mina. A few heavy bags and trunks are stacked in a corner. Mina is taking Van Helsing's good hand.

MINA:
You sure you'll be all right, Van Helsing?

VAN HELSING:
Somebody has to stay long enough to close out Seward's affairs. I owe him that much.

MINA:
We all do.

A moment of sad, shared warmth. Then, Jonathan comes in with another bag.

JONATHAN:
This is the last one!

VAN HELSING:
Besides, a few months in a vamp-free beachside town? It'll be a holiday.

MINA:
Pity you can't enjoy it in better health.

VAN HELSING:
Broken ribs, fractured arm, missing teeth. I've been worse off.

JONATHAN:
(jovially) You're no Lady, Van Helsing.

VAN HELSING:

(*a bit stiffly*) Nope.
You're cheerful, Harker.

JONATHAN:

I'm relieved to get back to London! Back to business!

VAN HELSING:

Yes. Never stops—does it?

> *A slightly weird moment.*
>
> *He shakes her hand; she takes it stiffly; there is some weird, slight, unspoken tension between them.*

JONATHAN:

Mina—I'll hail us a coach.

> *He kisses her cheek and exits. Van Helsing watches him, then:*

VAN HELSING:

—what about you, Mina Harker? What are your plans, for the rest of your life?

MINA:

You know. Matrimony. Motherhood. Maybe a bit of gardening.
I am done with adventure!

VAN HELSING:

This work, Mina—if it calls you—it is your responsibility to answer.

MINA:

Oh, no—

VAN HELSING:

I think you have a gift for it.

MINA:

—because I killed one vampire?

VAN HELSING:

One very old, very powerful vampire. Compared to him, the rest would be—

MINA:

Easy?

VAN HELSING:

—never easy. Still. Sometimes it's—fun.

MINA:
You really are mad, Van Helsing.

VAN HELSING:
Here *(she flips out a stake, and holds it out to Mina)*—take it.

> *Mina still will not take it.*

Just in case.

MINA:
In case of what?

> *Jonathan re-enters.*

JONATHAN:
Got one! I'll load the bags.

VAN HELSING:
Can you handle them all, Harker?

JONATHAN:
(grinning) I'm remarkably strong.

> *He exits; he is indeed handling the bags with ease).*

VAN HELSING:
—Mina... there's something—
(she doesn't know how to start) You know, I was—a bit like you, once. Married—and if not totally fulfilled—raised to be a Lady and accept my lot. My husband offered me stability; comfort; protection—in return, I only had to give him my life.
And then—
It started with little things. Mood swings. Temper tantrums. Wanting to command and control me. It built and built until—one night, he—came after me. *(she indicates her scar)*

MINA:
What did you do?

VAN HELSING:
It was him or me.
I chose me.

> *She makes a very deliberate motion with the stake—through the heart.*

MINA:
—he was—a vampire?

151

VAN HELSING:
I want to believe that those creatures are parasites; I don't want to think—that it is a natural evolution of the worst parts of human nature. That any—all men could turn dangerous if given too much power.

MINA:
What are you saying?

VAN HELSING:
Dracula is gone—but Jonathan's scar from the silver has not faded. And your husband still claims not to remember so many things—including how he escaped! *If* he even escaped, if the infection isn't still living on—in a new host!

MINA:
He can't remember because Dracula was erasing his memory!

VAN HELSING:
What else might he have erased?!

MINA:
He proved himself that night in the church!

VAN HELSING:
He showed some resistance—can we trust that he was never complicit?

MINA:
I can trust him, Van Helsing!

VAN HELSING:
(*she nods, then*) I have seen a man I thought beyond suspicion—turn before.
If it is destroy, or be destroyed—

> *She holds out the stake, to Mina.*
>
> *Jonathan pops his head in.*

JONATHAN:
Mina!

VAN HELSING:
You shall know him—by his acts.

> *Van Helsing holds out the stake. Mina looks at her, and hesitates.*

JONATHAN:
Mina! We're going to be late!

Mina takes the stake, and holds it.

MINA:
—Coming, dear.

She exits; holding the stake—pointy end out.

The End.